Retire On One Property Deal

How You Can Sky-Rocket Your Profits with Bigger Deals

Barry Davies

Mozaique Publishing
Carmarthenshire UK

ISBN 978-0-9576277-5-8

A CIP catalogue record for this book is available from the British Library.

I dedicate this book to my amazing wife Rupinder and to our first child who is due to be born in a few months' time.

Contents

Foreword.......... vii

Introduction ix

Getting the best out of this book ix

Part 1 My Story: September 2014 – February 2015 1

Chapter 1: Life Ain't All Sunshine And Rainbows 3

A Rude Homecoming 5

Why Me? 10

A Change in Business Circumstances 14

Ongoing Negotiations 16

Doing the Right Thing 18

Chapter 2: What Doesn't Kill You Makes You Stronger 20

Buying Ben Out 23

Chapter 3: A New Home 27

Chapter 4: Retire On One Property Deal 30

Valuing the Property 32

Estimating the Cost of the Works 32

Funding 35

"The Best Revenge is Massive Success" – Frank Sinatra 44

Part 2 How To Get Out There And Do It Yourself 45

Introduction 46

Chapter 5: Why You Should Do Big Deals 47
The Magic of Thinking Big 47
Mind the Ego 52
What does it take to be a Big Deal Investor? 54
Summary 57
Chapter 6: Back To Basics 58
Calculating Return on Investment 59
What is Yield, and is it a Good Way to Assess a Deal? 60
Return on Cash Left in the Deal 61
Summary 61
Chapter 7: The Devil Is In The Detail 62
Summary 69
Chapter 8: Hidden Profits 70
Hidden Gold Case Study: Fishponds, Bristol 73
Summary 78
Chapter 9: Maximising Your Investment 80
Do Single Rooms Rent? 84
Increasing Value through Converting Rooms and Extending the Property 84
Lease Option Case Study – Eight-Bedroom House (Five Rooms En-Suite), Harbourside, Bristol 85
Summary 88
Chapter 10: Recycle Your Cash 90
Getting the Best Valuation 91
Summary 93

Chapter 11: Dealing With Risk.. 94
Assessing the Risk 94
Mitigating Risk 96
Elimination 96
Reducing the Risk... 97
Quick List of Potential Risks 98
Don't Bet Everything You Have on a Deal 99
Always Have a Buffer 99
Insuring Your Property... 100
Perceived Risk vs. Actual Risk...................................... 101
Summary.. 103
Chapter 12: Creating A Support Network 104
Building a Great Power Team 104
Summary.. 113
Chapter 13: Financing Deals – Mortgages And Bridging Loans.. 114
Mortgages – is Interest Only Best or Should You be Paying Down the Capital too?... 114
Fixed Rate or Variable Rate 117
Bridging – is it Too Expensive? 118
Interest Risk and Stress Testing.................................... 119
Summary.. 119
Chapter 14: Attracting Funding For Your Deals 121
Borrowing to Invest 122
So When is it Right to Borrow Money to Invest?............ 123
Creating Joint Venture Partnerships to Invest 124

Steps to Ensure You're Building a Robust Portfolio 126
Marketing for Joint Venture Partners 126
Why JV? Isn't it Better to Keep All of the Profits? 127
Exit Plan 128
When Not to Joint Venture 128
Joint Venturing to Gain Experience.. 129
Tim's Deal 130
Icing on the Cake 134
Joint Venture Check List 134
Systemising the Process.. 135
So You Have Decided that a Joint Venture Partnership is for You – But How do You get Started?... 135
Summary... 142
Chapter 15: Investing With Others And Making It Safe 144
Do You Have Time to Do it Yourself?.................................... 144
Who to Invest with 145
Summary... 152
Chapter 16: Get Out There And Make It Happen........................ 154
Your Next Steps – Putting it all into Action............................ 154
Stage 1 – Make a Plan 155
Stage 2 – Get it in Your Diary 155
Stage 3 – Get an Accountability Buddy................................... 155
Stage 4 – Create a Power Team... 156
Stage 5 – Get a Mentor 156
Stage 6 – Find Your Hidden Treasure 156

Stage 7 – Get Out and Find Your Next Deal 156
Stage 8 – Organise Your Funding.. 156
Stage 9 – Get it Refurbished/Converted 157
Stage 10 – Get it Rented 157
Stage 11 – Get it Refinanced 157
Stage 12 – Find the Next Deal 157
Extra Resources 157
Summary.. 159
Chapter 17: Accelerate Your Success.. 160
Case Study – Mark's Deal, Lease Option in Cardiff................. 160
Educate Yourself 164
Retire On One Property Deal Seminar (Live One Day Event) . 166
Big Deal Mentoring Programme.. 166
Get in Touch 170
And Finally … 171
Action List 173
About the author 175

Foreword

I've known Barry for over eight years now and his journey in property has been a remarkable one, from humble beginnings to being a major player in the competitive Bristol property market.

Barry takes a "no bullsh*t" (pardon my language) approach to property and communicating what's really achievable. He genuinely tells it warts and all so from reading this book not only will you learn from his many successes, you can also avoid some very costly mistakes.

Don't expect a rose-tinted view of the world of life as a successful property investor. Yes, the trappings of wealth are there for those that do what Barry has done but this is a real life view of what it takes to "make it".

Seriously, if you are into property or even thinking about investing, read this book. Make notes and then read it again!

Ant Lyons
Editor

Your Property Network Magazine

Introduction

The last year has been a crazy time for me with many great highs but also some very low lows. I have written this book so that you, the reader, can replicate my successes and learn from my mistakes.

Getting the best out of this book

This book is a follow on from my first book *Escape the Rat Race with Property Lease Options*, in which I talk through my introduction to property and how I went from being sacked and broke in a recession to becoming financially free with a monthly profit of £7,500. That book and my approach at the time focused on the Rent to Rent strategy and on using lease options to secure high cash-flowing Houses in Multiple Occupation (HMO's). I highly recommend reading this book first, as I won't be covering these strategies in anywhere near as much detail here. By way of a thank you for buying this book I would like to offer you a digital copy (PDF) of *Escape the Rat Race with Property Lease Options* for free: you can get this by visiting ...
www.retireononepropertydeal.co.uk/ratrace.

With both books it's a great idea to take notes of key learnings; more important still is to make an action plan as you go through, detailing how you will use what you learn. Whoever said "*knowledge is power*" was mistaken. Knowledge is only potential power – action is where the power is. I didn't write this book so that you would have some nice bedtime reading; this book was written to help you become financially free, or rich even, if that's what you desire, but the buck stops with you. It is only you who can do it. Take notes, but more importantly take action!

Check out my website for more free resources and up to date case studies:

- Register For Free Resources and Information
www.retireononepropertydeal.co.uk/free

- Get The "Escape the Rat Race with Property Lease Options" Book
www.retireononepropertydeal.co.uk/ratrace

- Watch The "Retire On One Property Deal" Webinar
www.retireononepropertydeal.co.uk/webinar

- Take A "Big Deal" HMO Tour
www.retireononepropertydeal.co.uk/hmotour

- Find Out More About The Home Study Courses
www.retireononepropertydeal.co.uk/homestudy

- Receive "Big Deal" Training With Barry
www.retireononepropertydeal.co.uk/training

- Apply For 1-to-1 Mentoring With Barry Davies
www.retireononepropertydeal.co.uk/mentoring

Part 1

My Story: September 2014 – February 2015

Chapter 1: Life Ain't All Sunshine And Rainbows

"Life ain't all sunshine and rainbows. It will beat you to your knees and keep you there permanently if you let it. But it ain't about how hard you hit. It's about how hard you can get hit and keep moving forward; how much you can take and keep moving forward. That's how winning is done. Now, if you know what you're worth, then go out and get what you're worth. But you gotta be willing to take the hits, and not pointing fingers saying you ain't where you wanna be because of him or her or anybody. Cowards do that and that ain't you. You're better than that!"

Sylvester Stalone in *Rocky*

We had just been to Ibiza – a surprise thirty-third birthday present from my girlfriend (now my wife) Rupinder. This had been one of four holidays I'd taken that year, totalling six weeks abroad. I had worked really hard for this and was just starting to enjoy the fruits of my labours. I was driving from the airport back to Bristol, to a beautiful home I had spent two years creating.

That home was a big house in Clifton, the most affluent part of Bristol, on which I had signed a lease option contract two years earlier. At the time of signing the option agreement the house was almost derelict. It was a 165-year-old house that hadn't been touched in forty years. A couple had lived there until they had passed away a few years back, then a young family bought it intending to bring it back to life. However, they had failed to get the planning permission they wanted to extend into the roof as this was a conservation area. Following this, the husband had suffered a rare form of septicaemia after cutting his finger in the garden. His condition was so rare that the doctors didn't know how to treat it; he was given antibiotics but they did not work, his condition worsened and he ended up in intensive care on the verge of death. Luckily a specialist from Germany was able to prescribe the right antibiotics, and saved his life. Following the failure to get planning permission, and this horrific incident, this couple with their two young children decided that life was too short and gave up on the idea of refurbishing the house due to the huge amount of work required.

They put the property on the market for sale. Four years had passed since they had bought the house and in that time the global financial crisis had hit. Banks were no longer willing to lend large sums of money on properties in this condition. A buyer was found but their bank refused to lend.

I first saw the house whilst viewing another on this stunning crescent in Clifton. The property was ideal for a lease option because the sellers weren't willing to sell at a loss; with a lease option I could offer them more money as long as they were willing to wait for the funds whilst I refurbished the property. We agreed that I would lease it whilst I did the work, and then buy it for £375,000. The reason I was willing to do this was that the property would be worth £550,000 once I had spent £80,000-£100,000 refurbishing it. Therefore I would have a great profit and the owners would get what they wanted for the property.

There was a lot more work than anticipated and the property ended up costing £125,000 to renovate, and to convert the basement into a self-contained flat. We extended the option contract as this would be mutually beneficial – we had more time to complete the project and the sellers would benefit from not having to pay early redemption fees on the mortgage. To avoid those early redemption fees, we agreed to buy the property between 6th September and 6th October 2013. This gave us just a one-month window, but this was fine for us as we would be able to organise the mortgage before this time. We rushed to get the house ready for a survey and when the mortgage offer came through in August, I called the sellers to arrange the purchase. There was no answer but this was not unusual – the husband was often away on business. I called again a few days later; still no answer so I dropped them a quick email to arrange the details of the purchase. In the meantime my wife had arranged the trip to Ibiza on 7th September. It was a great surprise and a well-earned rest after all the hard work with this and other houses. Whilst we were in Ibiza the seller rang but noticing we were abroad said that we'd talk on my return. On the drive back to Bristol, I started returning the calls I'd missed whilst I was away.

A Rude Homecoming

I called the seller who told me that the option had expired as we should have served the notice before 6th September! My heart sank; surely this couldn't be true? My attention to detail isn't great, but I had read through the contract in detail at the time and remembered the key dates – I had to buy the property between 6th September and 6th October. Assuming the best of people, I suggested that we could still buy the house as the mortgage was all in place, etc. Surely this guy wasn't trying to screw us? I had become friends with these people, we had sat down and drunk tea, even had a beer together – we had a great relationship. Then my worst fears were realised. After I suggested we could still go ahead as planned, his response was, "*we are not really inclined to do that.*"

The rest of the call was a bit of a blur. About a million thoughts a second seemed to be rushing through my head. What was it they wanted? Another £10,000? Maybe another £20,000? Surely they wouldn't try to screw us for the lot? Where did we stand legally? Surely there must be a way to stop this? I think we must have agreed to meet or talk later that week; it's all a bit of a blur now.

Two or three minutes earlier, everything had been great. The house was finally finished, we had had an amazing weekend … but that was now a million miles away. I called Rupinder. Neither of us could believe what had happened. We both felt the same: "*Surely these people can't be that evil? There must be a way around this*."

This was the last deal that I was doing with Ben, my previous business partner. It was a 50:50 deal but Ben had since moved on to a new coaching business and now had very little to do with property. With a fledgling business and a new family, this was the last thing he needed at this stage in his life. Our plan had been for me to buy Ben out of his share of the house, and he would use his share of the profit to pay off debt that he carried from when we started the property business. I wanted to fix the issue before I called him so decided to call our solicitor next. I was still optimistic that we might be able to get around this, or that it would just cost us a few grand. My solicitor said that if the option had expired it would be hard to fight and he wasn't sure what our chances would be in court. It would depend whether we had a reasonable judge who would suggest that we needed to be reimbursed for the work, or whether the judge would see it purely as a commercial contract which had to be followed to the letter. What was unclear was whether all that we had installed belonged to us or to them. Our view was that it belonged to us. I decided that I would have to call Ben. This was not something I could easily fix on my own as I had done with some things in the past.

Ben was as shocked and gutted as I was. I tried to reassure him that it would probably be ok, but in my head was still struggling to understand how seemingly decent people could be so mean. These people were middle class, and had lived on a beautiful bohemian crescent where you couldn't leave the house without chatting to one or more of the neighbours.

The owners requested that we make them an offer to buy the house or for them to give us a consideration for the works we had done. We were still optimistic that we could come to a deal even if it ended up costing us a few more thousand. In the long run a few thousand wouldn't make a massive difference to us – it would be a lesson well learned and a mistake we would certainly not make again. We reluctantly offered to pay an extra £20,000 for the house, a big blow as we had already massively overspent on the project. Alternatively we offered to return the house to them if they paid us £165,000 (£125,000 to cover what we had spent + £40,000, which would form two-thirds of the profit – we had done the work after all).

We received a blunt reply stating that our offer was nowhere near what they wanted for the property. The husband of the couple who owned the house eventually agreed to meet with Ben and myself. Since he was coming alone without his wife we thought it best to write a letter explaining our relative positions. The total potential financial loss (£180,000 between us, i.e. £90,000 each, including what we had spent and the potential profit we were set to make) was more of a massive setback and inconvenience than a catastrophe for me as I had built up a strong property business with great cash flow. But I had put my heart and soul into this place; I had been running my property business during the day and often painting and working on this house during the evenings. I had lived on a building site for two years and really stretched myself financially. I had worked night and day to create a beautiful home in the best location in Bristol, and just when the dream was complete it was going to be snatched away.

For Ben, it would be a financial catastrophe. He had just started a family, and had taken the brave step to spend his life following his passion through his coaching/counselling business. Ben had been through the pain of setting up a property business with me, both of us starting with no money, but he left before it became really profitable (please read *Escape the Rat Race* for more on this). He had now started over from square one with a new business, and at this point was making enough to survive and live a simple life, hoping that the profits from this last deal (when I bought him out) would clear his debts and give him a few grand for a rainy day. If the worst happened, Ben would be left with £35,000 debt from this property on top of the £30,000 debt he already had and would risk bankruptcy. He was about to get married, and now faced having to cancel his honeymoon and scale back the wedding. Needless to say, this was the last thing he needed.

We detailed all of this in a letter and waited for the owner to arrive. We were both very anxious. When he turned up for the meeting, accompanied by someone we had never seen before, I was shocked; he looked ten years older than the last time I had seen him just a few months earlier. It was now a grey-faced, gaunt man who faced me when I opened the door. Was he ill? Was he dying? Was this the reason he needed the money so badly that he was going to try and double-cross us for it? It would be half understandable if this were the case, if he would be leaving his wife a widow and his children fatherless. I invited him in. He introduced his friend but didn't explain why he was there. I think he had been too scared to come alone to tell us what he was about to say. Ben suggested that we all took turns to speak rather than arguing or speaking over each other, which was a great idea as with tensions running so high this could have easily turned into a shouting match. The owner explained that this was simply a business decision and that he was just doing what was right for him and his family. He talked almost like we were corporations screwing each other over contracts, with no personal consequences. He was trying to convince himself as much as us; he was shaking as he spoke and looked like he was about to expire.

As it turned out, it wasn't that he was seriously or fatally ill and needed the money. When it came down to it, his greed, and/or his wife's greed, was telling him to do something that nearly every cell in his body knew was wrong. This, perhaps, was what made him look so grey and gaunt, as if he were fading away.

Ben described his own situation: his young family, the business he had just started. He explained he was getting married in two weeks and would have to cancel his honeymoon. He also said that this may mean bankruptcy for him; that the interest on the loans was high and he had been biding his time until the project was complete, so that he could pay his debts off when my mortgage came through on the property.

When my turn came to speak I explained that I had put two years of my life into this house, restoring it lovingly to its original beauty. I had often worked fifteen hour days, and weekends, to bring it all together. I had stretched myself financially and had spent £125,000 of borrowed money to turn what was a complete wreck into a dream home. My girlfriend had just given up a well-paid job in London to move here and this would make us homeless. I explained that we planned to make this our home and wanted to start a family there – and if we were to do that we needed to do it very soon as time was running out for us. Losing our home and all this money would cause a lot of stress and could ruin our plans. To us, this certainly was not just a commercial transaction.

It all fell on deaf ears. He hadn't come to listen; he had come to say his piece. It's very likely he was just the messenger for his wife. One problem we had was that he couldn't have known whether we were telling the truth or not – most people would say anything to save £125,000 that they had worked so long and hard for. The sad reality was that we had both accurately described our situations and hadn't overplayed anything.

The meeting lasted only fifteen minutes and it was the weirdest fifteen minutes of my life. I have never met someone in such dis-ease. The biggest argument that day, I believe, was an inward one within this guy's head, which we weren't party to. The word disease is derived from the French word *desaise*, which is made up of *de-saise* – lack of ease. No wonder this guy looked so ill. Could money be so important to someone, that they will not only screw people over but also go against their own values and beliefs to the extent that all the blood drains out of the face, making the person gaunt and grey and causing them to tremble with every word they utter?

Before he left he asked us to make another offer to buy the property or to return it in exchange for a financial consideration. My emotions were now running very high. There was no way we were going to give the place back in a great condition – I would sooner have ripped out everything I had painstakingly put into it and walk away with nothing than give it away for a pittance. Logically of course this didn't make sense, but … this was my home and I felt he was trying to steal it from me.

Why Me?

I couldn't help but wonder, "*Why is this happening to me? What have I done to deserve this?*"

I have always done my best to help people and have a positive effect on the world as much as possible, in the small ways that I can. Half of the profits of my first book were going to the NSPCC – my favourite charity. I had run the Brighton marathon and the London Marathon for the same charity, raising thousands. I was also donating blood platelets every single month; even when I was working fifteen hours a day I would always find the two hours needed to do that. So from my perspective, all this seemed so unjust. Here was I, donating blood platelets month in month out; meanwhile this guy who (it felt to us) was trying to screw us had had septicaemia (blood poisoning), and countless blood transfusions to save his life. That blood would have come from someone like me. The irony would be funny if it weren't so painful. Usually when people have a near death experience and nearly lose everything they realise what's important in life, become grateful and become better people, yet this event had seemed to come and pass without effect. If anything it seemed to have caused more greed and less compassion.

I was feeling very sorry for myself. This, I thought, as the matter festered in my mind, shouldn't be happening to me, a guy who tried to help others wherever he could. My mind flashed back to a time during the project when I went running around the docks near the house, something I did two or three times a week at around 7.00 am. On one cold winter's morning whilst on my run, I was deep in my thoughts, running through what I had to do that day. As I ran towards the M Shed Museum on the dockside, I saw two men looking rather animated. They flagged me down as I approached and asked if I could swim. I was so deep in my thoughts that this question sounded utterly abstract and completely threw me. What a weird question! Who were these people? What did they want?

"*A man has fallen in the docks*" one of them said with urgency. "*Neither of us can swim.*"

I still wasn't sure if these people were serious or joking. This type of thing just doesn't happen in real life, does it?

In a split second my mind, as it tried to assimilate what was happening, was searching my memory bank and sprang back to a program I used to watch called *999*, where situations like this were re-enacted for a TV program. My mind was darting all over the place. I think I was in shock.

"*He's already been in there two minutes*," he yelled. "*We need to get him out. Can you swim? CAN YOU SWIM?*"

I looked down and saw a guy floating face down. Shit! This wasn't a joke or a reconstruction. This was actually happening!

I stripped off to my boxer shorts, ready to jump in. The guy was floating between the side of the docks and a ship that was moored up. The water was about three metres below the dock we stood on, and the gap between the dock and the ship was about one metre. There was a cast iron ledge that ran the length of the ship and jutted out about six inches. The last thing I wanted to do was knock myself out as I jumped in.

Carefully, I jumped in to the water and managed to roll the guy over. He looked grey and his glasses were still half on his face. I put myself underneath him and held him above the water. He was fully clothed and had a rucksack on; he was very heavy.

What now?

Shit! I hadn't really thought of that.

The guys on the dock said that the emergency services were on the way. We needed to get him out of the water.

But how?

One of the other guys jumped down onto an old tractor tyre that was floating on the water between the dock and the ship, acting as a buoy, and between us we managed to lift this chap on to the tractor tyre. Then, we were able to drag and swim the tyre to a floating wooden jetty about 25 metres away. We could hear sirens and by the time we lifted him on to the jetty, the ambulance had arrived and the paramedics took over. A small crowd had by now gathered on the dockside.

I watched as the paramedics worked and worked to save his life. Somebody threw me down a blanket – I was standing there in my boxer shorts, dripping wet, in the middle of winter. It was probably cold, but I wouldn't have known with all of that adrenaline running through my veins.

Somebody took me inside the museum. Again I heard the sirens as they left to take this chap to the hospital.

Tragically it was too late. They had not been able to save him.

They took me to the hospital too, to do an ECG and some other tests. They offered me counselling as well, but there was no need. I was fine. I had done all I could and didn't feel responsible. This was just a tragic accident. I was home before 9.00 am, ready to start work.

Thinking back to this event, I couldn't work out why it seemed I was about to be made homeless. Was there no justice in the world? No Karma? I wasn't just some money-hungry property developer who would trample on whoever he had to to make his fortune. I often went out of my way to help people, in this case even putting my own life in danger to try to help a complete stranger. I did my best to be a decent guy, living and working with integrity. If this was the result, it seemed bloody unfair.

But there was no point in Ben and me feeling sorry for ourselves.

We would have to battle to save this house. Painful as it was, we offered to buy the property for £410,000 (£35,000 higher than the option price). This would give the owners over half of the profit that I had worked over two years for. Alternatively we said, if they wanted the property back we would accept £160,000, which would cover the £125,000 spend and give us half the profit.

They replied, saying that if we wanted to buy the property we would have to pay £515,000 (the original price agreed was £375,000); or alternatively they would be prepared to pay us a consideration of £40,000 to walk away and return the house to them in a perfect state. Having spent £125,000 on the property and increased its value by £185,000 we felt this was outrageous. There was no way I was willing to accept this. I wanted to tear the property apart brick by brick and undo all of the painstaking work I had put in to it. That would be excruciatingly painful – but not as painful as being cheated by these people. Obviously it would cost us dearly; tearing the property apart would mean that we wouldn't get the £40,000 offered, and Ben and I would be left £125,000 in debt between us. Somehow that still felt better than giving away this beautiful house.

A Change in Business Circumstances

There was another problem – Ben and I had different views on the situation. Ben had not been around and had not worked on the project so was not emotionally involved. Naturally he just wanted to walk away with the best possible financial position for his family, a much more mature way to look at the situation rather than letting pride and ego take over. I, on the other hand, had put everything I had into this place to make it my home. I didn't want to be bought and was willing to walk away with nothing rather than let someone else benefit from all my hard work for a pittance.

The reasons for our differing views were a result of the different levels of involvement we had had in the project, and our differing circumstances. Initially Ben and I had moved in to the property together to do it as a joint venture (as we always had with all our projects) but I knew his heart wasn't really in it. He had already started his coaching business and was focusing more and more on that. After we had been living there a couple of months, Ben was staying at his girlfriend's house more and more, then eventually moved in with her. This was when he decided to leave our business to focus on coaching.

In the meantime, we had established our office at the house and Melissa, our lettings manager, came there to work every day. As I was there all the time, all her questions, all the decisions and the overall responsibility for the letting business inevitably came to me. In addition, the house had needed a complete refurbishment and we were converting the basement into a flat. I was always on site, so all the questions from the guys about the work and materials on the project also came to me.

At the same time I was mentoring others, the profits of which were going straight into our joint business. (For six months after Ben left, £15,000 from my mentoring activities continued to go into the joint business.) All in all, with the property portfolio, the lettings business, this large conversion and the mentoring I was working sixty to seventy hours a week. In fairness, Ben tried to pick up some property mentoring clients to do his bit, but wasn't as successful. He wasn't active in property any more so it was a hard sell for him.

From then on, I decided to take my mentoring work outside of the business and do it personally for myself. Since we were sharing the profits of this last project 50:50, Ben also agreed to help out more with the house but with a young family and a new business it was hard for him to find the time. Since this was the last deal we were doing together and because Ben was like a brother to me I was happy to still split it 50:50. At this stage though, I decided to step back from the manual work but still oversee the overall project. The agreement with Ben was that my girlfriend and I would buy him out of his share of the house/maisonette at £375,000, sell the basement flat at £175,000, and split the profits of that 50:50.

When the deal looked like it was turning sour I felt really bad for Ben because I knew it would hit him really hard financially. However, I also felt that since Ben would have been taking 50% of the profits despite me doing 90% of the work, it was only fair that he took 50% of the loss if it went wrong.

Ongoing Negotiations

Negotiations with the owners of the property seemed to be going nowhere, then someone suggested that it might be a good idea to use a mediator to come to a resolution. They agreed to this and a date was set. Since Ben and I had very different views on the situation, we needed to work out a way forward between us before going into the negotiation. Ben didn't want to walk away £65,000 in debt; I didn't want to sell my soul by giving the property back for a fraction of what we had spent on it. The owners had offered us £40,000 to walk away, which I was unwilling to accept, but because I didn't want to have to buckle in the negotiation due to Ben wanting to accept a low offer, I offered Ben £20,000 to walk away, which he could then use against his half of the debts. I could then go into the negotiation alone and if successful, would get the house. If not, I would end up with all of my half of the debt, and over half of Ben's debt from this deal too. Ben decided not to accept this offer. We were and still are very good friends and he didn't want me walking away with nearly £90,000 of debt whilst he would walk away with £45,000. We would go into the negotiation united, ready to walk away and remove everything from the house if necessary.

The mediation consisted of us being in one room, the owners in another, and the mediator going between us. The sellers put the story to the mediator that we were not in a position to buy the house, which was why we had not exercised the option. We were able to prove to the mediator that we had contacted the owners to discuss completion on numerous occasions; we had had a mortgage survey done and were in a position to buy. He became a lot more positive and his whole energy changed, he seemed to think this had perhaps been a misunderstanding that would get resolved. He went back to their room to discuss this. When he returned the look on his face said it all. There was no misunderstanding. These people were just trying to screw us. They increased their offer to £70,000, which was just over half what we had spent on the property. The meeting was a waste of time. Maybe it had been naïve to believe it could be anything but a waste of time. We left the meeting completely dejected. We were back at square one.

That evening I started removing the kitchen from the basement flat, and organised for our lock-up to be cleared so that we could fill it with the kitchens, bathrooms, heating systems, carpets, etc. The next day Ben called me to ask me to reconsider the offer as he was worried about all the debt. This was exactly the position I didn't want to be in and exactly the reason I had offered him the £20,000 to walk away. Although I understood his concerns, I was disappointed that he had changed his mind just twenty-four hours later. Since I had already offered him a way out I didn't really want to back down, and he did accept this which I was really grateful for.

The option contract had now expired and the only thing legally keeping us at the property was a tenancy agreement that had previously been put in place to satisfy the sellers' mortgage company. This was due to end two weeks later. It was now the end of November and this had been going on since the beginning of September. Living in the house that I had lovingly restored should have been an absolute joy but in these circumstances it was hell. Every morning the sun would pour in through the gorgeous big bay window, across the oak and granite kitchen I had always dreamed of. Close friends wondered how I coped during this time, but I couldn't really see what other option I had.

Doing the Right Thing

I wondered whether I was doing the right thing. The money was one thing, but I was also facing potential criminal damage charges. Although I had paid for everything the owners were now arguing that this formed part of the house and belonged to them. This pissed me off but nothing they did surprised me anymore. I was caught between doing what I felt deep down was the right thing to do – tearing the house apart – and doing what would serve me best going forward. On the one hand I felt that there was no way I should let people do this to me; on the other I knew that the best thing going forward might be to just let it go. I could either spend the next twelve months paying off a massive debt, potentially being prosecuted and maybe sued for criminal damage. Or I could spend it paying off a smaller debt, but most importantly building my already successful property business.

Usually I am very decisive, but this time I really didn't know which way to turn. Was my pride really worth that much? Did I want to spend the next year in and out of criminal and civil court? Was I really thinking of letting these people get away with this?

One morning I finally decided that I wanted to spend the next year building the business and moving forward in the most positive way. I hated that I had been screwed over by these people, but I would be screwing myself over further if I had to spend the next twelve months with court cases hanging over my head. It killed me to call and tell them that I'd given up, that they could have the house back.

Once the call was over, I felt strangely liberated. I felt able to move forward. The owner, however, continued to be a complete pain in the a**e, wanting to deduct £100 from his offer for this and £100 for that. I had little energy left to argue. Moving out of that house was one of the most depressing things I have ever had to do. It was the middle of December and we should have been spending our first Christmas in a perfect home. Instead I was putting my stuff into storage and preparing to live between my Mum's house and my girlfriend's.

This was the last thing I expected at the age of 33.

Chapter 2: What Doesn't Kill You Makes You Stronger

"Life is 10% what happens to you and 90% how you respond to it."

Lou Holtz

Even before the deal on my home was settled, I decided that I wouldn't let it affect me adversely. Even if the worst outcome was realised and we lost a load of money and my home, I was determined I would still come out on top.

Whilst we were going through hell I kept my eye on the goal and a great deal came up. To be honest, working on the new property deal was a very welcome distraction from this draining and depressing situation. The property was a 12-bedroom HMO (House in Multiple Occupation), a deal brought to me by a contact who lived outside of Bristol. Somebody had visited his website about HMO's and contacted him. The following is a case study of the deal that I wrote at the time:

Case Study: Monster HMO, £1,500 Profit, Rent to Rent

As an HMO lease options specialist, one of the perks of the 'job' is the deals that come your way from people outside the area or people less familiar with lease options or HMO's. I was delighted that when

I was sat sipping a cup of tea in a coffee shop in Bristol, I got a call from a contact who had a lead for a 12-bedroom HMO just around the corner. My contact had mentioned lease options to the owner briefly but left the negotiations to me.

I visited the property – a large former care home – then sat down with the owner to discuss the situation. She had owned the property for a number of years and run it so successfully that she had been able to retire off the proceeds some years back. She then leased it to another company who ran it successfully as a care home for a number of years, but that company fell into financial difficulty. The lady decided to rent the property to students and obtained an HMO license for twelve people. Completely inexperienced in this field, she leased it to sixteen- to seventeen-year-old students from a local college, all of whom were part of an American football team. I'm sure you can imagine what kind of experience she had in the six months before she was able to get rid of them …

It was at this point that she started considering her options, and phoned my contact who put us in touch. We knew we could rent the property out for £4,000-£4,500 without doing a massive amount of work. I proposed a lease option, offering to lease it for £1,800 a month for up to six years with the option to purchase the property at that point for £500,000, which was the current market value.

Unfortunately the landlady was nervous about tying herself into a long term contract due to the experience she had had with the previous (care home) tenant going bankrupt, and then the last lot trashing the place. In the end we agreed to lease the property for three years for £2,000, with an informal agreement to be given first refusal on the purchase of the property. Unfortunately the price was not fixed so it would be hard to get a good price. It would have been great to have the legal option to buy the property but she would not budge on this.

We signed the lease and took over the property. There were only two bathrooms so we reconfigured two of the disabled toilets to add showers. The property already had two kitchens and heaps of communal space. Since we didn't have the legal option to buy it at a fixed price, we did not want to spend too much on refurbishing. It was slightly dated but clean, so was fit for tenants. The only extra money we spent was £1,000 to replace the old single beds with double beds.

The property was fully rented within nine days. This is how the deal stacked up for us:

Lease fee	£2,000
Bills	£750
Management (employee wages @ 8 hours a month)	£80
Maintenance	£100
Total cost	£2,930
Total rent	£4,435
Monthly profit	**£1,505**

Our costs

Finders fee	£3,000
Addition of two showers (installed into existing disabled toilet rooms)	£2,000
Furniture (already furnished but replacing single beds with double beds)	£1,000

Legal fees	£700
Deposit (refundable at end of lease term)	£4,000
Total cost	£10,700
ROI	**191%**
Total profit over three years after all costs	£54,180

I did this deal whilst still negotiating on the property that I was living in, and it really rejuvenated my spirits and helped me get some confidence back. The £1,500 per month would also massively help me move on financially and clear the debt more quickly. With this small win behind me, and the ongoing support of my lovely girlfriend, I was ready to smash some more deals and put the setback firmly behind me. Although I had made a monumental mistake I was still in the game. I started to realise it had been a blip rather than a catastrophe. I had a very successful portfolio and was still financially free – albeit with a big chunk of debt to pay off.

Buying Ben Out

During the previous couple of years I had felt solely responsible for the business. Although Ben and I were still joint owners of a number of properties, whenever there was a problem I took it upon myself to deal with it; as a joint business, it wasn't really working. Ben was not shirking his responsibility – it was just that I hated asking him for any money when I knew he had a young family to feed. One example was when the boiler on one of our properties broke down and I didn't have the heart to call and tell him he owed me £600-£700 for his share. I didn't resent this as I had cash flow coming in from other properties that I had bought without Ben, so it didn't really affect me that much, but at the same time, since I was continually investing in new properties, I never felt particularly flushed with cash so it did add a little pressure.

After we lost the deal in Clifton, Ben's circumstances changed. He had been biding his time until the profit came through from the Clifton property so that he could pay off his existing debts. Now he had been lumbered with a load more debt. We had managed to pay off some of the debt to our investors with the funds from the settlement received from that property, and this did ease the burden. We were negotiating with our investors who were very understanding but at the same time wanted their money back. Some of that debt was secured against another property in our portfolio and we really didn't want to lose that house too. Ben and I agreed to split the debts 50:50. Ben was pretty much sick of property by this point, whereas I still strongly believed in it as an investment since my other properties were doing well.

To help Ben to pay off his half of the debt, and help me build my portfolio, Ben and I discussed me buying him out of the properties that we had together. Since we were only just coming out of the recession there was only £20,000 of equity in the first property: £10,000 of that was mine and £10,000 Ben's. I decided I wanted to keep this one if at all possible. I also had £22,000 debt outstanding to my girlfriend who had invested in the Clifton property but she kindly agreed to wait for her money so that I could buy Ben out. I committed to buying him out within four months so he could repay an investor who was chomping at the bit to get his money back, as the funds were now overdue.

This meant that I now had to find £10,000 to buy Ben out, on top of paying off my debts and continuing to do new deals. After two months I still didn't have the funds together as I was paying off other investors, but I knew I could do it. During that last month I worked hard on both my property business and my training business and somehow managed to pull together £9,000. (Even during this really tough time, I managed to expand my portfolio.) Ben owed us £1,000 from something else so that £9,000 was enough to buy him out. I breathed a massive sigh of relief.

It worked well for both sides as Ben really needed to get his debt paid down; he didn't want to sell the assets he had in his own name as he wanted to keep a bit of a pension. That £9,000 was enough for him to pay off his most eager investor and keep the wolf from the door for a while.

I really felt for Ben during this time, with his young family and fledgling business, and considered helping him pay off some of his debts. The truth was I still had debts of my own from the deal that went bad and had already paid £15,000-£20,000 of joint business costs out of my own pocket by this time, largely without his knowledge. I realised that considering paying someone else's debt when you still have your own … is a little crazy!

The properties that we owned together were not the best – we had bought them before I realised that the most important thing when buying properties is cash flow. When we started investing, in our naïve and optimistic early days, we would buy a property just because it was cheap and we thought it would go up in value. It didn't really bother us that it didn't make much money; we thought we could weather that. We had bought one property with a joint venture (JV) partner's funds and it hadn't really increased in value at all. What's more, since we were paying them interest every month, we weren't making any money on it either, and whenever there was a problem, we had to fund it out of our own pockets as there was such little profit. In the end, we decided to sell this property as the JV partner wanted her money back and it wasn't worth buying her out.

On one hand it was a shame to lose one of the properties from our portfolio but on the other hand at least the liability was gone and we didn't have the worry of things going wrong and costing us money.

Chapter 3:
A New Home

I was still living between my girlfriend Rupinder's house 120 miles away, and my Mum's house. It was a depressing state of affairs. I was thirty-three years old and pretty much homeless even though I had a portfolio of properties. Rupinder and I looked around at rental properties for the short term and were horrified at what we saw. We had always hated the idea of throwing money away on rent and when we looked around, the standard of accommodation we saw was not great even if we spent £1,500-£2,000 a month. Rupes and I were also in the process of buying a property on which Ben and I had signed an option contract four years earlier. We had agreed to buy Ben out and were planning it to be an investment property, but since we were struggling to find suitable accommodation, Rupes suggested we move into this one instead.

The property was run down when we signed the option and since we had agreed to buy the property at 90% of the market value after four years, refurbishing it during the lease period made no sense as it would have increased the value. Although it was a beautiful house in a great area, I wasn't keen to move in. I had lived there before and it seemed like a step backwards. The problem was that our alternatives were worse – £1,500 pm rent for an 'ok' 2-bedroom flat wasn't appealing at all.

We decided to go ahead and move in though, because we knew we could make it into a nice home in the short term, then sell it at a good profit when the work was complete and we had somewhere else to go. Luckily for us, we had agreed the price before the market had really started to pick up.

The property was valued at £326,000 because it was in need of work, which meant that we could buy it at £296,000 in line with our option contract. During the time we were buying the property, the house next door sold for £390,000 and shortly after we moved in, the property directly opposite sold for £492,000. At last we had some luck, we were on to a winner! ... or at least we thought we were. We applied for a mortgage but even at this low price the surveyor said that since it was a bit run down and the sash windows needed to be replaced in the near future, the bank should not lend on it. We were in the shit *again*. How could this happen? Hadn't we had enough bad luck? The option on this property was also due to expire so we had to act fast.

Somehow I managed to delay the sale for six weeks whilst we did the work. We replaced the windows, replastered a lot of the walls, fitted a new kitchen, new bathroom and even fitted a downstairs toilet. We worked tirelessly to get this finished, sometimes with up to ten guys working in the house at once. We had booked the survey in for four weeks later to allow us to get the mortgage through, and the week before the survey we worked fourteen hours a day. Our plasterer/jack-of-all-trades, Darren, also worked twelve hour days to help us get through it.

The night before the survey we were up until 3.00 am, then up again at 5.00 am to finish off. All of the main work had been done in the first two weeks but we didn't want to leave anything to chance. We crossed our fingers and waited for the surveyor. The house wasn't 100% finished but surely it was close enough? We only needed to get it valued at £296,000, which was almost £200,000 cheaper than the house across the road. Rupes and Darren the plasterer went to the café, and I waited nervously for the surveyor. I'm not religious but I'm sure I prayed that day that another home wouldn't be taken away from me.

The surveyor turned up and looked around. He seemed satisfied that the house was renovated to a good standard although some parts weren't quite finished. I didn't fully trust him as he was the one who had down-valued it the previous time. I wanted to know for sure, so asked him directly: was there any reason that this house might be down-valued? No, he replied, he was happy with the standard of the house and would report this back to the mortgage company.

I was so relieved and completely exhausted when I showed him to the door. We had done it, no more commuting from Hemel Hempstead to Bristol to work! No more worrying about where I was going to live. The icing on the cake was that we would be living in a house for which we had paid £296,000, but which was worth £425,000-£450,000. At long last our struggles and efforts from starting a property portfolio with no money and living on the breadline were starting to pay off. Finally we were getting some lucky breaks.

This house was in an area with great pubs and a trendy high street, and all my friends lived just a stone's throw away. I went to meet Rupes and Darren in the café and gave them the good news. We were all exhausted and I felt like I could sleep for a week. Darren didn't even ask to be paid for the overtime he had worked, although we made sure we paid him for every hour and gave him a bit of a bonus too. Having a great team is so key to being successful, and we are very lucky to have such a dedicated bunch of guys.

Chapter 4:
Retire On One Property Deal

As soon as we completed the twelve-bedroom Rent to Rent deal, another great opportunity came along: a large commercial property three minutes' walk from Cabot Circus, a £500 million shopping complex in the centre of Bristol; and in the same postcode as the headquarters of all the major banks and insurance companies that employ young professional workers in the city. From merely looking at the floor plan, it was easy to see it could accommodate up to twenty large bedrooms, many with en-suite bathrooms. In this area these rooms, which would be more like studios with sofas, etc., included, would achieve high rents.

The property had started out on the market for £440,000 eighteen months earlier, but while we were working on the large Clifton home project, it was too much to take on. Luckily for us, the sale of this property fell through twice over that eighteen month period because other investors hadn't been able to raise the funding. The problem with the property was that it would either have to be bought with cash or with a bridging loan. Neither high street banks nor commercial lenders would lend against a large empty commercial building in need of work and with no income. High street banks would be unlikely to lend on a property of this size (generally they won't lend on HMO's with more than five rooms); commercial banks on the other hand are happy to lend on cash-generating properties of any size. This though was in need of work and not generating income. I considered development finance but this would be very hard to get on a project with no planning permission.

For these reasons, the other parties had failed to raise the finance. Eighteen months had passed since the owners had originally put the property on the market and they were keen to sell. Over that time, the asking price had come down from £440,000 to offers in excess of £360,000. To put this into perspective, this is the price of a three- to four-bedroom house in Bristol. With that price reduction, this deal started to look very interesting. I instinctively knew that it would be very profitable but did some rough calculations to prove that. Using the floor plan I worked out that I could create two six-bedroom flats, one four-bedroom, and one three-bedroom flat. By looking at the room sizes, I could see that at least twelve of those nineteen bedrooms were big enough to have en-suite bathrooms, and from this I was able to work out the total rent based on very conservative rental figures.

Double en-suite rooms: 12 x £525 =	£6,300
Double rooms: 7 x £420 =	£2,940
Total monthly rent =	£9,240

Our management is done within our company by our own Lettings Manager. We allocate a cost of £130 per HMO per month, therefore:

4 x £130 =	£520

Maintenance varies greatly but we assume £100 per HMO per month, therefore:

4 x £100 =	£400

Utilities bills are made up of fixed costs such as council tax and broadband, and variable costs such as electricity and gas. Therefore we assume £200 fixed costs per property + £40 per tenant for the variable costs, so:

6 bed =	£200 + (6 x £40) =	£440
6 bed =	£200 + (6 x £40) =	£440
4 bed =	£200 + (4 x £40) =	£360
3 bed =	£200 + (3 x £40) =	£320
Total bills =		£1,560

Valuing the Property

A commercial bank would value the property based on its income minus the bills:

£9,240 - £1,560 = £7,680 per month = £92,160 per annum

Generally in the Bristol market, banks/surveyors will value a property at ten times rent (net of bills) – this is the equivalent of a 10% yield. Therefore this property, based on conservative rents, would be worth:

£92,160 x 10 =	£921,600

Estimating the Cost of the Works

This was a healthy valuation – especially since the property was on the market for offers in excess of £360,000. These numbers were getting really exciting! All we needed to do now was estimate the cost of the works. We had recently converted a five-bedroom house into an eight-bed with five en-suites including a small rear extension for under £40,000. If this was the cost of refurbishing and extending a large Victorian house surely each flat wouldn't cost more than £50,000, even including the fire and sound proofing? This would give a total cost of £200,000. Admittedly this wasn't the most scientific approach, but it gave a good ballpark figure and I was getting too excited to go through all of the details of the works. By this point I knew I had to have this property and wanted to put an offer in. Before I did, I finished my rough calculations:

Valuation	£921,600
- Offer	£350,000
- Works	£200,000
= Instant Profit/Equity!!!	**£371,600**

We knew we wanted to keep the property long term so wanted to work out the mortgage costs and profit. The banks would lend 70% of the value:

£921,600 x 70% =	£645,120

So we should be able to borrow £645,120 against an asset that would cost £550,000 to buy and renovate. This meant that we would get all our money back + well over £90,000 cash-back on top. This sounded too good to be true. I rechecked my calculations. Then when I still didn't believe it I called my broker. He confirmed the figures.

Assuming the mortgage would be about 6% (commercial mortgages are more expensive than normal buy-to-let mortgages), the mortgage would be:

Mortgage amount:	£646,800
x interest @	6%
/ months	12
= monthly mortgage payment	£3,234

Next it was time to work out the potential monthly rental profits:

Rent:	£9,260
- monthly mortgage	£3,234
- bills	£1,560
- management	£520
- maintenance	£400
= profit per month	£3,546
= profit per year	£42,552

So once this deal was complete we would get **£96,800 cash-back** through the remortgage.

We would then make **profits of £42,552 per year** after all costs!!!

I was now getting really excited about this deal. Then I had to remind myself that I didn't actually own the property yet, didn't have finance lined up, and there was no planning in place. I managed to get my feet back on the ground – just! By this point I knew I had to make this deal happen somehow. It would dwarf the debt I was facing on the property I had lost.

To buy this building we would have to overcome two big challenges: (i) we would have to find a way to fund the project and

(ii) we would have to get planning permission to turn it into HMO flats.

Funding

After eliminating high street lenders, commercial lenders and development finance, it seemed that our options were either to buy with cash, borrow the money from a private investor, or use bridging finance. We didn't have the funds to buy the whole property in cash ourselves so that wasn't an option. We considered trying to find the money from other cash rich investors but didn't know anyone who wanted to invest a lump sum that big into a deal. We thought of taking out multiple smaller loans but this can be quite hard work with a lot of administration; also there would be legal costs for each loan so this would not be a cheap option.

We wanted to act quickly so decided to pull together as much of our own cash as we could and take out a bridging loan for the rest. The main problem with bridging finance is that it's bloody expensive – often 12%-18% per annum! There are frequently set-up fees and exit costs too. Bridgers will usually lend up to 70% of the property purchase price, and want you to put in the rest from your own funds. So this is how the deal would work with a bridging loan:

Purchase price:	£350,000
Deposit (30%):	£105,000
Bridging loan (70%):	£245,000
Monthly interest (1.5% per month):	£3,675

This was going to be very expensive. Remember that on top of the high monthly interest charge, the legal fees (your own and the bridger's) and the survey fee would come to roughly £5,000; set-up fees of 1%-2% and exit fees of 1%-2% would also often be incurred. A deal like this can cost tens of thousands in legal and bridging fees. This can be enough to put most people off but then most people aren't rich so you don't want to follow the masses. Would you make the sacrifice of paying a few thousand a month in the short term if the reward was a few thousand a month profit for the rest of your life? Even with this huge potential most people still wouldn't have the balls.

I'm not saying you should be ruthless and take massive risks. That would be foolish. But you would be wise to remember that it's hard to achieve much without taking some risks. The key is to assess the risks and mitigate them. In this case, the risks were:

- That this big monthly interest cost would put pressure on our monthly cash flow, which would make us less stable financially and could cause us to run out of money if we faced a number of other challenges at the same time. Anyone in business knows that there can be lots of ups and downs.
- That we might not get planning permission for the conversion and could end up with a building that we didn't know what to do with.
- That the works would cost more than what we anticipated and would lead to us running out of money.

With the big financial hit of losing my home I knew it was crucial to get this right as we couldn't afford two big failures. We needed to go through every risk to find out a) how likely it was to happen and b) if it did occur, how severe would the consequences be?

The financial pressure it would add to our monthly finances was significant. £3,675 was a lot of money to find for the interest payment every month. What risk did this pose to our business?

Well, over the last few years we had built up a significant monthly cash flow through the deals we had done, so we knew we could afford this monthly cost. I also had the income from a successful mentoring business to add to it, which would help. The only question was: could we afford this and any other unforeseen costs that might come in?

When you have a number of properties there is always a chance that some big costs could come in, and although for the last couple of years our occupancy rates had been 98%-99% with no non-payments, we couldn't assume that this would always be the case. Overall, with the strong monthly income from properties and the extra from mentoring I was comfortable with the risk level. We were already putting money aside for maintenance every month and had a rainy day fund. Based on these factors we didn't feel that this was too great a risk.

The risk of not getting planning permission was quite unknown. Although the property was in a regeneration area (a positive) it was also in a conservation area, which could sometimes complicate things. We read local planning policies and felt fairly confident that we would get planning permission. When applying for planning though it often seems that you are at the mercy of planning officers' whims; if they are having a bad day you might not get it. This made me uneasy. We needed a Plan B in case we did not get permission to convert the property into four HMO's.

I knew that the planning laws at the time had been relaxed so that offices could be converted into residential units without having to go through the full planning process; it could be done via the prior approval process instead. This relaxation of planning law had been brought in to encourage development to improve the economy, therefore there seemed a fairly good chance that our application would go through. I did some sums though, and as six two-bedroom flats the property would actually be worth more than as four HMO flats so this was a viable option. We wanted to keep the flats long term and our priority was monthly rental profit/cash flow so four HMO's remained our preferred option as the rental profit would be £1,500 more per month with this configuration.

Although plan B was more likely to go through, there still seemed to be a chance that the council could find a reason to object, and again this made me a bit uneasy. What if we didn't get planning to do either? Was there a plan C? Preferably one that didn't involve planning whatsoever?

Looking at the size of the building and the price of it, I realised that even with no planning permission we could refurbish the property and rent it out as office space for a profit. This would have been less profitable and harder to achieve as we had not done it before, but it worked well as a plan C. Now we knew that even if the worst came to the worst it would still be profitable. With this in mind I was comfortable in moving forward.

The obvious next step was to put an offer forward subject to planning permission. This would eliminate the risk of owning a property for which we could not get the required permission. I called the estate agent and offered £350,000 subject to getting planning permission to convert the building into flats.

Unfortunately the agent said that if the seller had to wait until we got permission they wouldn't go lower than £400,000. We considered our options and because we had a Plan A, B and C, we were confident enough to relinquish our insistence on getting planning before moving ahead. We offered £350,000 with three months between exchange and completion so that we wouldn't need to pay an expensive bridging loan for too long whilst waiting for planning permission to come through. The offer was accepted and we were in business! We were over the moon with the deal and couldn't wait to get started.

The next step was to exchange contracts and apply for planning as soon as possible so that we would not be paying expensive finance costs for too long. We knew there was a lot riding on gaining permission so decided to get an expert planning consultant to give us the best possible chance of getting permission granted first time without having to go to appeal. Even the consultant said it was an unusual case and she hadn't dealt with anything similar before. This would not be one HMO, it would be four, and she wasn't sure how to position the application.

We decided to go straight from commercial to HMO without converting it to residential under the relaxed planning laws. We pulled the application together relatively quickly, got an architectural surveyor to draw up the plans, submitted the application, crossed our fingers and waited, and waited … and waited.

It was scheduled to be a three-month process during which the consultant stayed in constant communication with the planners, offering support and answers whenever needed. But even after the three-month period when the decision was due, we didn't get a response. This was highly frustrating as the property was now costing us a fortune in interest. We had paid good money to the planning consultant but she seemed powerless too. In the end she wrote to the Head of Planning and various other bosses within the council who then set a new deadline: the decision would be made a full five months after the application was submitted. Again this was highly frustrating. We felt as though we were caught between a rock and a hard place. Either we could wait patiently and pay a fortune in interest or we could give the planners hell and get on the wrong side of them. Although this shouldn't affect their decision we really didn't want to risk it.

The planners' decision came a full five-and-a-half months after we had made the application – two-and-a-half months late! But it was well worth the wait. We were granted exactly what we wanted – nineteen bedrooms over four flats.

Meanwhile we had been busy buying and renovating two houses – one with seven bedrooms, the other with eight – we had purchased in Southville, Bristol, a great area within walking distance of the centre of town. The seven-bed profited at £1,700 per month and the eight-bed at £2,100 per month. The cash flow of the portfolio was really picking up. This size of property was our new standard. The cash flow achievable on five- to six-bedroom properties just wasn't attractive anymore compared to these deals. Even these weren't exciting compared to the nineteen-bed though!

The next stage on the big nineteen-bed project was to get building regulations sign-off, a process that was much more straightforward and predictable compared with the planning process: if you meet the regulations you get the sign-off, you're not at the whim of the council like you can be with planning. Part of the process was to get structural reports done to ensure that the floors within the building were all strong enough. When the report came back it turned out that we needed eleven structural steel beams (steels) inserted through various parts of the building to support the extra weight of the sound and fireproofing. This would add some cost but nothing major in the scheme of things.

We chose to use a builder who had proved successful in structural works when constructing two extensions for us. We got the site cleared and started work on inserting the steels. As we ripped the place apart we started to discover some other problems and had spent £40,000 by the time we had the site cleared, inserted the eleven steels, and rebuilt some of the structural walls.

In the meantime, Rupinder and I took our eye off the ball slightly whilst we were off getting married and going on honeymoon. The builder working on the nineteen-bed project was also running another job for us on a seven-bedroom HMO with four bathrooms, which we were renovating for a friend. The day we returned from our honeymoon we had room viewings scheduled on the seven-bed (not that we were doing them – our Lettings Manager sorts out all of that). We landed and travelled straight back to Bristol, and arrived at the house to find that the double glazing hadn't been installed, the carpets hadn't been fitted and the property was still a building site. Twenty people were coming for viewings and we had to decide whether to go ahead or cancel them and reschedule. We had previously rented rooms in properties that weren't fully complete but this was on a different level entirely. However, we decided to press on anyway … and not one room was taken from the twenty viewings. To put this into perspective, the last two properties we had completed two and three months earlier had completely rented in ninety, and 120 minutes respectively. This was a disaster. Instead of relaxing and enjoying life as newlyweds, my wife and I spent the next week on site all day every day to put this right. By the following week the property was 97% complete and just about ready for viewings. We rented out four of the seven rooms following these viewings; the house took another four to five days to finish, and within this time the remaining rooms were rented.

Now that we had some breathing space we could assess the damage. The project had overrun by two weeks and the costs had overrun by £23,000. £13,000 of this money was extra works which we had accounted for, but that still left £10,000 of extra cost that couldn't be accounted for. Explaining this to the friend for whom we were buying this property was tricky; we ended up foregoing our sourcing and project management fee to reduce her costs, but since we had achieved such a great finish through the extra works the property was valued £20,000 higher than our initial estimate. This meant the investor still made a substantial equity gain, similar to what she had expected, and was also getting higher rents than expected.

Our bigger problem was that the builder who had managed this was also project-managing our big project. If we had an overspend proportional to the one we'd just had, it would cost us an extra £50,000-£100,000. We held emergency meetings to resolve the issue but the guy said it was impossible to predict the costs on a build this size. He's a good builder but we just couldn't continue to run the build with an open cheque book, not knowing how much costs might spiral. Reluctantly we had to let him go.

We now needed to find another builder fast. Our bridging loan, although affordable, was costing us a fortune. We got a recommendation from a friend and within two weeks had an initial estimate of circa £200,000. This seemed reasonable and we were happy to proceed, but the new builder said he needed to double-check his figures. We chased him for four weeks; each time he said he was finalising things but was still aiming for £200,000. A full six weeks after the initial quote we received the final quote of £320,000 – 60% more than he had originally said. Not only did the figure seem astronomical but we also felt we'd been messed around and no longer trusted the guy.

We were back at square one – over £3,000 monthly bridging loan costs and no builder. In desperation I turned to Facebook of all places, to try to get a recommendation. We got a quote from a friend of my brother but again it was over £300,000, which seemed really expensive (you could build three or four houses from scratch for that price). We weren't sure where to turn but explained there was no way we could pay that much. The builders said they really wanted the job and asked for some more time. They came back with a revised estimate of £260,000. With the money we had already spent this would take the total cost of development to over £300,000. There had been some changes (all nineteen bedrooms would now have en-suite bathrooms) but this still seemed like a lot of money. It was decision time: should we reject the offer and go back to the drawing board? We could continue to pay £3,000 a month in costs whilst we searched and even then there was no guarantee that we would get a better price. Bristol was really picking up, buildings were going up everywhere and the recession was a distant memory. Tradesmen were in high demand so the chances of getting this done for a lower price were fading. Although this was a lot more than we wanted to pay we decided to bite the bullet and give the builders the go-ahead. It was now nearly three months since work had stopped and it was great to get things moving again.

At the time of writing the project is coming to an end. Rents in Bristol are very high and we expect to achieve total rents of over £12,650 per month due to the increased number of en-suites and the increased demand in Bristol as a whole. The monthly profit will be over £6,000, so including the admin fees, etc. that we charge, we expect to generate an annual profit of £73,900 after all costs including management and maintenance.

The building has been given a preliminary valuation of £1,250,000 on completion by the bank's surveyor. Based on this figure, even with the overspend we will be able to refinance to get all of our initial investment back, plus £100,000-£150,000 on top because we have created so much value within the property.

"The Best Revenge is Massive Success" – **Frank Sinatra**

I'm sure you want to know how I settled the score after the debacle with the person who took my home away.

In the year since losing my home I have secured £2,875,000 worth of property. £2,227,500 of this is ours, with £647,500 belonging to joint venture (JV) partners. Our share of the equity created within these deals is £610,000.

I have increased our annual income by £174,400.

We are now looking for a new home having narrowly missed out on a couple of £1,000,000 properties in sealed bids.

We got married at the end of 2014 and are just thinking about starting a family. We couldn't be happier!

You see, it's not about them, it's about us. What happens to them is of no concern of mine. I could easily have let this event have a negative effect on my life, using it as an excuse why I couldn't do this or couldn't achieve that, but that would have been a bad decision. Each of us decides how events will shape our lives and it's essential that you decide the positive route. I made the decision to make this an amazing year and have surpassed all of my expectations. When I look in the mirror I can be proud of what I have achieved. I have grown wealthy beyond my dreams in so many ways. As for him, neither he nor we will ever forget what he did, how his greed was greater than even his own values. You can't judge a man by your own standards; everyone has grown up differently and had different influences.

Part 2

How To Get Out There
And Do It Yourself

Introduction

Hopefully, after reading about my property journey you are inspired and raring to go. As you can tell from my story there are a lot of potential pitfalls as well as the massive wealth potential that lies within property investment. In this section of the book, my aim is to guide the thought processes you should go through and the actions you should take to become a successful investor and move on to bigger deals where the profit is exponentially higher. To get the best out of this book, take notes, but most importantly make sure they lead to actions.

Chapter 5:
Why You Should Do Big Deals

"Believe big! The size of your success is determined by the size of your belief."

David J. Schwartz

The Magic of Thinking Big

As well as being a great book by David J. Schwartz, *The Magic of Thinking Big* is a great strategy. In this, David explains that the main difference between people who achieve great things and those who don't is in the way that they think. Somebody who thinks big will find ways to take advantage of an opportunity that comes their way, whereas somebody who thinks small will think of all the limitations and reasons why they can't do it. Doing bigger deals starts with thinking big and grows from there. There are lots of reasons why, in property in particular, it's a great idea to think big.

It's less crowded at the top

If you're looking at standard investment properties like one- to three-bedroom flats and houses you will have a lot of competition. Not only are most other investors looking for the same deals but so are first time buyers. People looking to get on the housing ladder are a lot more motivated than most investors and will often be willing to pay more, which makes it hard to get a house at a good price.

When looking at larger houses that you can rent as smaller five- to six-bedroom HMO's you can face similar challenges because you will be competing with families looking to increase the size of their home. These people will generally be willing to pay more than investors. One such property we enquired about recently attracted twenty viewings and nine offers within one week; it sold for £20,000 over the asking price. There are still some opportunities to get deals where the properties are in too bad a state for families to consider, especially if you can find ones that have no kitchen or no bathroom. Such properties are considered uninhabitable and therefore unmortgageable, and will be out of reach of most traditional purchasers. These can be secured using bridging finance and therefore can be a great opportunity for investors.

Existing large HMO's can be a good opportunity, especially if they have become tired over the years of multiple occupation. The fire doors, alarm systems and quirky nature of these properties will often put off owner-occupiers, and therefore they will generally be sold to investors. Cash rich buyers will often pay good money for properties in good condition that are ready to rent, and will produce a good income without the need for extensive work. Where these large properties are in a poorer condition, the cash rich buyers are often put off as they don't generally have the time or experience to put them right. These are the properties that can provide a great opportunity for investors in a position to refurbish them; they can be sold as investments and attract a price tag relative to the rent that they generate. Since such properties are tired, the rent will be considerably less than what is achievable with a newly-refurbished high-end HMO. Therefore there is an opportunity to buy these properties, fully refurbish them, add en-suites and charge premium rents. As a result, it becomes possible to achieve a much higher valuation based on the improvements made and increased rents, which will allow the investor to refinance and recover much of their investment. Typically on projects like this in Bristol, we aim to recover about 50% of the total funds we invest.

For more experienced investors there are bigger opportunities still. These come in the way of commercial buildings which can be converted into residential properties. Tired commercial properties may no longer offer viable office space. Less and less people require offices as more and more work from home, or even from coffee shops and so on. Advances in technology mean that people can work from anywhere where they can log on to the internet. With the gradual move to paperless offices few now even require a printer. Those who do rent offices require modern amenities, such as air conditioning, well insulated offices, electric points inset into the floor underneath desks, and so on. Modern offices are also generally open plan rather than a series of rooms as they used to be. Old buildings simply are not set up to provide the kind of service that people require. For these reasons it is possible to make a great investment with this type of property. Such deals are better suited to people with some experience, but if you have that experience and want to step up to the next level the rewards can be massive. Less than 1% of investors are working on these larger deals, so as you can imagine there is a lot less competition; there are less people looking for large deals that make a massive return on investment than there are looking for standard buy-to-let properties with a boring 6% yield. Whereas with a large HMO we would look to refinance a property to recover half of the money we invested, with large projects like this it can be possible to recover your entire investment (including deposit monies, all fees and refurbishment costs). In some instances, where you add enough value, it can even be possible to recover more than you invested, as in the example of our *Retire On One Property Deal* case study in the previous chapter.

You could retire on one deal

As you will be aware from the case study, it is genuinely possible to retire from just one property deal. Our best deal so far generates £58,000 profit per annum from nineteen rooms. We are now searching for a property that we could convert into fifty rooms across ten five-bedroom flats – we estimate that this could create in excess of £120,000 profit per annum.

You could build a massive income from just a handful of properties

Maybe £58,000 like our case study isn't enough for you to retire on. Our top six deals generate £170,000 profit per annum after all costs including management and maintenance.

Here is a handful of our best properties:

Our Top Six Properties

Location	**Profit**
Old Market	£72,085
Coronation Road	£25,932
Hotwells	£24,600
Gloucester Road	£17,331
Gloucester Road North	£20,094
Clift House Road	£25,932
Total	**£185,974**
Letting Fees	£6,200
Grand Total	**£192,174**

You can get disproportionately higher returns with big deals

Big deals can involve more work both in terms of going through the planning process and completing significant refurbishment or conversion. This extra work should be rewarded through the much larger profits that you will achieve, and the greater return on investment.

Once you have completed a deal it is common to refinance the property and borrow against the new higher value. With bigger deals it is possible to create a lot of value in the property; the bank will lend 70%-75% of that value allowing you to recoup much of your investment through borrowing more against the property. With small HMO's it's common to get a 20%-40% return on the capital you have tied up longer term. With big deals, getting a 50%-100% return on your money is common.

You can get your time back

Many people start investing in property to achieve financial freedom. If you need to build a very large portfolio based on mediocre returns to replace your income you could end up being anything but free. Investing in single let family homes that make £200 profit per month will mean that you may need twenty-five houses to replace a £60,000 salary. If you focused instead on larger, highly profitable HMO's you could replace that £60,000 salary with just three properties.

Investing in this type of property also means that you will be able to pay somebody else to manage and maintain them. Only when you have people in place to run your properties can you achieve freedom. I'm writing this book from the terrace of a hotel just outside Alicante in Spain, and since we have been here our Lettings

Manager has rented six rooms in a newly-renovated property and five rooms that became vacant elsewhere in our portfolio. We are able to manage the existing portfolio from anywhere in the world, and when we are in the UK we can focus our efforts on growing the portfolio and improving the business.

As you can see it really pays to think big and go for the big deals. Standard buy-to-let investments provide boring returns and the market is too overcrowded with amateur investors and owner-occupiers happy to pay big sums for small profits.

Mind the Ego

It has to be said, big deals are cool! It's great to be able to say that you have done a million pound deal but you need to be very careful: this is your ego talking – and it can really trip you up.

As I finished writing my last book I was embarking on my first million pound deal, a twenty-five-bedroom block of flats with two commercial units below. The property was on sale for £1,250,000 and I believed that it would be worth approximately £1,500,000 after a bit of refurbishment and splitting it into individual flats. I felt that the amount of people in the market for a £1,250,000 property would be small and this would hold the value down. By splitting the units, I considered that each of the flats would be worth £250,000; and the commercial units worth £80,000 and £120,000, making the total value £1,450,000.

Each of these flats would have become leasehold, and then the freehold itself would have a value as each flat would pay ground rent. On a property of this value the freehold would be worth £30,000, bringing the total value to £1,480,000.

My plan was to buy the property with bridging finance; split it into individual flats; and get a mortgage against the increased value of the sum of the leaseholds (£1,450,000).

On the basis that I could borrow 70% of £1,450,000 (£1,015,000), I agreed to buy the property at £1,175,000.

On the face of it, looking at the basic figures, we would have £160,000 tied up long term but would have a very large property in a prime rental area in the centre of Bristol. Most importantly I would have done my first million pound deal. The big problem was that there were a lot of costs involved:

£58,000 stamp duty

£16,450 broker fee (2% of the £822,500 loan)

£3,200 survey fee

£6,000 legal fees to buy and split

£83,650 in total

This money would have to be left in the deal along with the £160,000 originally calculated, meaning that we would have £243,650 tied up in this property long term. Because a lot of this money would have been borrowed from investors, our monthly interest payment would be higher too. When we took all of this into account our monthly profit after all costs would have been £2,200. Although this is a decent chunk of money to have coming in every month, compared to the size of the deal it was pretty small. Part of me (my ego) still wanted to do the deal but common sense prevailed and we walked away. My hunger for a big deal would have to wait.

What does it take to be a Big Deal Investor?

Diligence

Anyone who has read my first book knows that I am not afraid to take massive action – and some risks.

When I started investing I had no money and therefore nothing to lose. I found a way to invest with no money and used the lease option strategy to become financially free relatively quickly. That mindset got me a long way, but not always 'dotting the i's' and 'crossing the t's' has also lost me a lot of money – even my beautiful home as you learnt at the beginning of this book. When you are doing deals, it's essential that you are diligent to avoid mistakes like the one I made. With bigger deals the stakes are a lot bigger, the investment usually higher; although there is more money to be made, it is also possible to lose a lot of money. Therefore the most important thing you must do is to be diligent: check all contracts, check and double-check your figures, and make sure you get advice from the right people.

Massive hunger for success

Over the last few years I have mentored a lot of people and helped them build great wealth, yet there are some who don't take the action necessary to be successful. I have often pondered what makes some successful while others struggle to get out of the starting blocks. The one thing that I have found to be the greatest factor in someone's success, the most important factor, is the desire to succeed. I have mentored relatively wealthy people with good sums of money to invest, but who did not get the results that either of us wanted for them. Some of these people had comfortable lives, decent incomes and felt it would be nice to build a portfolio for extra – and importantly, passive – income. I have mentored others who struggled to find the money for the mentoring, or used credit cards to pay for it, and had little left to invest … yet these people have been some of my biggest successes. Is it the wealth that's a factor? I think not. It is the amount of desire that an individual has to be successful or to get out of their current situation. Those who thought it would be "nice" to develop an extra income have been infinitely less successful that those with a burning desire for success.

One of my most recent clients, Tim, invested in two great deals with us on the understanding that I would teach him through the deals. Tim and his wife are both doctors. I would consider them to be a relatively wealthy couple, but their problem (which spurred their desire for success) was that both of them found their jobs very stressful: they were seeing a patient every ten minutes and continuously being asked by the NHS to do more work for less money. Tim wasn't afraid to take action, and was very proactive and decisive. He took every bit of advice and ran with it. Because of his massive desire for success he learned very quickly. Within eighteen months he had managed to replace a doctor's salary – no mean feat. Using what I had taught him, Tim built over £100,000 of semi-passive income (we manage his properties for him) in just eighteen months. It had taken me about five years from buying my first property to achieve that.

Self-belief

Nowadays I talk about our successes from the stage to educate and inspire others to achieve similar results. After the talk many congratulate me on those successes, often asking if they can invest with us.

It's kind of easy to believe in myself now, but it was not always this way. When I was sacked and broke in the credit crisis in 2009 and I decided that I would never work for anyone else ever again everyone thought I was a bit crazy. Whenever I told friends of my plans, they looked a little dazed and confused. They weren't being nasty: they just didn't really think it was possible to grow a portfolio with no money. Whenever I spoke to my mum, she always said "*as long as you're happy, love*," and tried to hide the panic and nervous expression on her face. This is when you need to develop and maintain an unshakeable self-belief. If you truly believe in yourself deep down and are willing to do whatever it takes to succeed, nothing will stop you.

Take massive action

As important as the inner mind game is, unless you take massive action you will never be successful.

In today's competitive property market you may need to view fifty to one hundred properties to get the right deal. If you really want to fast track your success, you need to be constantly looking for property, looking for investment partners, managing refurbishments and also managing your growing portfolio. In the initial stages, unless you decide to invest your money with someone else who is doing this, property is far from a passive investment. As you grow you can hand over various aspects of your portfolio to other people to help but initially, to build the momentum required, you will need to be relentless in taking action.

Persistence

If you're going to have to view fifty properties before you get your first deal, it means you'll have offers rejected time and time again, especially if you're trying to structure the deal creatively. Viewing forty-nine properties that don't work in order to find one deal that does work is going to be tough even for those with strong willpower. You may even have some deals that fall through at the last moment after you've spent thousands of pounds on legal and survey fees. This is when you really need to dig deep and keep going. So many give up at this point and never reach their full potential or achieve financial freedom. If you can pick yourself up and keep going you will get a reward; if not, you'll have gone through all of the pain for nothing. There were so many times in my journey where it would have been easy to give up but I simply refused.

Summary

Doing bigger deals starts with thinking bigger.

Make a goal to make each deal bigger and better than the last. The best way to financial freedom is through doing bigger deals. It's so much better to have three properties that make £2,000 profit per month each, rather than thirty that make £200 per month each. Let's face it, if you had thirty properties, you would have created another job for yourself rather than financial freedom.

Because less people do bigger deals, they are significantly more profitable. Our five-bedroom properties make a profit of £100 per room per month, whereas our ten-bedroom properties make a profit of £250 per room per month. This means the five-bed might make a profit of £500 per month compared to the ten-bed making £2,500 per month.

Your next deal doesn't need to be a massive HMO; just make sure that you are heading in the right direction. If you invest in single lets, then double your profit by making your next deal a small HMO; if you're investing in six-bedroom HMO's, double your profit by making your next deal an eight-bedroom HMO.

Chapter 6:
Back To Basics

"*Gentlemen, this is a football.*"

Vince Lombardi

The passage below was written by Charles Swindoll, and I don't think I could put it better myself …

The late football strategist Vince Lombardi was a fanatic about fundamentals. Those who played under his leadership often spoke of his intensity, his drive, his endless enthusiasm for the guts of the game. Time and again he would come back to the basic techniques of blocking and tackling. On one occasion his team, the Green Bay Packers, lost to an inferior squad. It was bad enough to lose ... but to lose to that team was absolutely inexcusable. Coach Lombardi called a practice the very next morning. The men sat silently, looking more like whipped puppies than a team of champions. They had no idea what to expect from the man they feared the most.

Gritting his teeth and staring holes through one athlete after another, Lombardi began:

"Okay, we go back to the basics this morning ..."

Holding a football high enough for all to see, he continued to yell: "Gentlemen, this is a football!"

How basic can you get? He's got guys sitting there who have been playing on gridirons for fifteen to twenty years ... who know offensive and defensive plays better than they know their kids' names ... and he introduces them to a football! That's like saying, "Maestro, this is a baton." Or, "Librarian, this is a book." Or, "Marine, this is a rifle." Or, "Mother, this is a skillet." Talk about the obvious!

Why in the world would a seasoned coach talk to professional athletes like that? Apparently it worked, for coaches don't lead their teams to three consecutive world championships all the time. But how? Lombardi operated on a simple philosophy. He believed that excellence could be best achieved by perfecting the basics of the sport.

So before you get out there chasing monster sized deals, it is important to master the basics.

Calculating Return on Investment

Return on investment (ROI) is simply the amount of profit you make in a year compared to the amount of money you invest. So if you invest £100,000 into a deal and the profit is £12,000 a year (£1,000 a month), you can work out the ROI by dividing the annual profit by the investment you've made.

Therefore:

£12,000 / £100,000 = 0.12

To make this into a percentage you simply multiply the result by 100:

0.12 x 100 = 12% ROI

What is Yield, and is it a Good Way to Assess a Deal?

Yield is a measure of how a much a property rents for in relation to its value. The yield is calculated by dividing the annual rent a property achieves by the value. If a property is worth £200,000 and you rent it out at £1,000 a month, you calculate the yield as follows:

£12,000 (£1,000 rent x 12 months) / £200,000
= 6% gross yield

Ideally you would want to find properties with a high yield as these are more profitable. Unfortunately high yield properties are often in less desirable areas with less desirable tenants. Investors are often willing to accept less profit to own properties in better areas. Your goal is to secure properties in great areas and increase the yield by developing the property and maximising the rent.

The problem with yield is that everyone calculates it differently. Some calculate yield before costs such as insurance, management and maintenance. I have even seen some agents advertise yields for HMO's and not include the council tax and utility bills that the landlord pays. This spurious calculation of yield artificially shows the properties to be very profitable. Because there are so many ways of calculating yield, this measure is often manipulated by the person trying to sell the property. So is yield at all useful? Yes, it can be a useful measure of a property, but only if you calculate it yourself and are consistent with the way you work it out. If you do this you can use yield to compare one property against another.

Return on Cash Left in the Deal

My favourite measure of whether a deal is any good is the return you get on the funds that you have tied up in a property for the long term. Generally I will buy a property, refurbish it and then refinance it to withdraw as much of the investment as possible to invest in the next deal. Unless the deal is outstanding you will still have some cash tied up in it longer term, so measuring the return on the cash left in is the best way to judge a deal. Ideally of course you would want to work this out before you buy a property. You can do this by estimating the cost of works, the rent achievable and the potential value of the property once complete. If you know the value of the property you can work out the size of the mortgage and the amount of your cash that you will get back when you refinance.

Summary

It's essential to get the basics right. As they say on Dragons Den – "*You've got to know your numbers!*" This is especially key when dealing with bigger properties. Getting the numbers slightly wrong can result in large financial costs since every mistake is amplified on big scale projects. Numbers aren't everyone's forté; this is ok, you just need to get some help from someone who is hot on numbers. Either get somebody to teach you the basic principles covered in this chapter or, if that's too tricky, team up with someone who can help you analyse your deals.

Chapter 7:
The Devil Is In The Detail

Knowing the details is critical in any business. I should know! I lost over £100,000 for not reading a contract properly. This I why I was so glad when my girlfriend, now wife, Rupinder decided to join the business. Her attention to detail is second to none when checking contracts and also when dealing with numbers. Rupes pretty much runs the business now, meaning that I seem to be able to just have fun all day – by this I mean I go out finding properties, finding investors, writing books and running the mentoring side of things. I enjoy this side of things so much that it doesn't even feel like work to me at all and would do it even if I didn't need the money. (Oh, actually I don't need the money and I still choose to do it!) Rupes really enjoys keeping everything working in order and managing the team and the portfolio whereas doing what I do wouldn't float her boat at all. She's so good at what she does I have asked her to share her top tips on running a successful business.

Here's what she had to say in her own words.

I purchased my first investment property in 1998 and went on to buy another five properties in the next twelve years. It was a slow journey for me as I was investing alongside a demanding job and managing the properties myself. I started to find that the more successful I became at work the less time I could carve out to dedicate to my property hobby. Back in 1998 it had seemed easy when I had nothing to lose, but as the years went on, investing became more and more complicated, the mortgage market completely changed, TV programs made investing more popular and the market become more competitive. Now, with capital and some equity behind me, I had something to lose.

Because of these changes I actually needed to dedicate more time to property than before if I was to get it right. I needed more time to conduct the amount of viewings required to find the very best deals, to carry out all the necessary due diligence, to do the financial scenarios, and to manage any refurbishments. It was this lack of time and the associated risk of getting it wrong that led me to reconsider my investment strategy. Although I had the funds for property investment, I did not have the time for it so I decided to look for a joint venture (JV) partner who had the time I lacked, but more importantly the expertise and a successful track record.

This is when I came across Barry and initially started working with him. We JV'd on a deal where I provided the funds for a property he sourced and refurbished. We then refinanced to recoup ALL of my investment. This was the first of many great things to come between us!

A couple of years later when I joined Barry's business I found it had a great work ethic and a real creative energy. There were lots of good things happening, resulting in fast growth and the team worked really well together to get done whatever needed doing. However, there was an overall lack of processes, organisation, and best practices. Although too much of these can add bureaucracy and hinder the growth of a business, this needs to be balanced with what is efficient and safe; by working smarter a business can improve efficiency, reduce duplication, increase staff motivation, and improve overall profits. During my first few months I started to implement some of the structure and processes I felt were lacking. The five items I've listed below had the biggest impacts and they can easily be adopted in your business.

1. ***Aim to receive all rents on 1st of each month, rather than tenants paying rent throughout the month.***

   Some landlords set up tenancies so that the tenant pays rent on the same day of the month they moved in; for example if they moved in on the 10th of the month, they pay rent on the 10th each month. Imagine having fifty or more tenants all paying on various dates throughout the month. How would you know if any had missed their payments? Perhaps by cross-referencing a list that you had created of payments due, however this would be time consuming and is not an efficient way to operate.

   If a tenant moves into one of our properties on the 10th, we take partial rent to cover 10th-31st, and then the full rent becomes payable on the 1st of each month thereafter. The benefits are numerous: you don't have to continuously check the bank account; any missed/late payments will become obvious quickly; you will have the rents in before paying any of the costs (see point 2 below); most importantly you will save time and mind space.

2. ***Set up a window for outgoing payments between 1st-10th of each month.***

   With the exception of council tax and water bills which have to be paid on the 1st, we set up all the regular outgoing payments between 5th-10th. This includes mortgages, lease fees, utilities and broadband. The reason we do this is so that by the time payments start to debit our accounts, the rents have already been received therefore mitigating any chance of missing a payment and incurring unnecessary bank fees. Missed payments may also impact your credit rating therefore it's very important to make every payment on time every month. By managing the dates yourself rather than leaving it to the suppliers, you are ensuring you set things up to best suit you.

In addition to the above, we also receive other invoices throughout the month for non-regular payments such as maintenance bills, etc. For these we operate two payment runs: one on the 15th and the other on the 30th of each month. Again this means we do not have to engage our time making payments throughout the month.

3. ***Have a dedicated bank account for your properties.***

When you first start out it is easy to use your personal bank account for receiving rents and making any property-related payments. However I would recommend opening a dedicated account just for your investment property as soon as you acquire your first one. When you have a handful of properties, you could still use a personal account instead of a business account if your bank is happy with this, but when you get to five or more properties I would recommend opening a dedicated business account.

The reason for having a dedicated account, be it a personal or business account, is that it allows you to have a record in one place of all your property-related income and expenditure. Completing your tax return is much easier if your records are easily accessible and up to date. Imagine if your rental income and expenses were mixed up with your personal expenditure: you would need to go through a year's worth of account statements to identify the property-related items. With a dedicated account you could even pass the bank statements straight over to your accountant who would be able to work through them without too many questions.

4. ***Create a Profit and Loss statement for each property.***

Depending on the number of properties you have this can become a time consuming task, so I'm not saying it is one that you need to complete yourself; I'm just saying it's something that should be done to enable you to see the profitability of each property, or not!

A profit and loss (P&L) statement is a summary of the revenues and expenses generated by a business over a given time period (monthly, quarterly or annually is most common). It reflects past performance and is used to track how a business is performing.

The basic equation on which a P&L statement is based is Revenues - Expenses = Profit.

Having a P&L for each property gives you powerful knowledge to help you make the right decisions. If this is not done regularly it is difficult to know the levels of profit each property generates. With a P&L you can rank your portfolio in order of profit, you can identify the cash cows, you can compare expenditure levels between the properties and identify if any are unnecessarily high, which could highlight a potential issue.

Log income and expenditure by property each month to create a P&L rather than waiting until the end of the tax year. However if you can't do this monthly then quarterly is the very least you should do. You may want to start off creating your own P&L on a spreadsheet but if you lack the time or knowledge, or as you expand, it may be worth considering using a book-keeper to produce these for you because it will be more efficient. The important part is not the data entry but what the numbers tell you.

5. ***Stay on top of property maintenance.***

As your portfolio grows so will its maintenance requirements. There is no getting away from it; if you ignore outstanding maintenance issues they will not go away and probably will get worse, so acting quickly will not only deliver a good level of service to your tenants, it will likely save you money.

As we manage a large number of properties, we operate a maintenance log. Onto this we record the details of the issue along with the date it was reported. One member of our team is responsible for keeping this document up to date, and we review the list each week. We aim to resolve issues within certain timeframes we have set, depending on severity. We sometimes use our own maintenance team to carry out the repairs and other times appoint a contractor. When using external contractors we always try to check the repair is completed sufficiently prior to settling their invoice. It is too difficult to get someone back to rectify poor workmanship once they have been paid. It is good practice to let contractors know you pay your invoices twice a month and they will get paid on the next payment run. This way they won't start chasing you as soon as they've emailed you their invoice. Once a job is complete we note it as such on our maintenance log.

If you have two or three properties you may not need a log, however with any more than this I would highly recommend keeping a record. It means you won't forget or leave any issues unresolved, and you can stay on top of them. You will also be able to refer back to it if an issue recurs, which could raise alarm bells as to the quality of the repair initially completed.

The above five changes are not rocket science, but they have had a significant impact on how our business now operates. As a team we have become more organised and professional, as we have records we can refer to rather than rely on memory. We have become more efficient with our time as some of the time-consuming and recurring tasks have been reduced or eliminated. This has resulted in each team member becoming more effective in their own roles, and allows each of us to focus on getting things done rather than administration.

If you are like Barry, who doesn't personally enjoy setting up processes and would much rather be out there finding deals, then find someone else who is passionate about it, and get them to do it for you. Being organised and working smarter ultimately leads to a better working environment and increased profits, so putting in the time to set these things up correctly is a sound investment in the future of your business.

Rupes has given a rather nice version of what she walked into when she joined the business. In reality, she found unpaid parking tickets and even a few overdue bills, unopened post, and management accounts that were far from up to date. Basically, although I had the key things covered, I was really poor on the details and it was costing me both in cash terms and mind space. It's important to get the details right. This will be natural for some of you reading this, but for others like me it is far from easy. Don't worry if this is not your strength, you just need to get someone on your team who is great with details. We'll cover this later when we discuss building your power team.

Summary

The details are very important and it's essential to take care of them to ensure you don't make the mistakes that I did. If you set the processes and procedures up correctly when you start, you will save yourself days or even weeks of time in the long run, and also save yourself a fortune.

Chapter 8: Hidden Profits

"*You are, at this moment, standing, right in the middle of your own 'acres of diamonds'.*"

Earl Nightingale

Many of the people reading this book are likely to have already made investments in property. Let's face it – like me, you probably didn't do everything perfectly the first time round. The good news is that you could be sitting on a fortune of hidden profits, as I found I was.

If you haven't already done this, it is probably about time you carried out a review of your existing properties. Are there single lets that could be multi-lets? Are there 3m by 4m bathrooms crying out to be converted to double bedrooms (assuming you can fit a small shower room in elsewhere)? Do you have a loft that could be made into two double bedrooms, possibly without the need for planning permission? Could you extend the property 3m to the rear to create an additional bedroom? Again this could be done without planning permission.

In Bristol, where I invest, a double room will rent for £425-£475 per month (£5,100 per annum based on £425) and an en-suite double room will rent for £525+ per month (£6,300 per annum). Let's assume that £500 of that annual rent money will be used up by increased utilities bills: that means that for every extra en-suite double room we create, we get an extra £5,800 in annual profit, and for every double room we would get an extra £4,600 annual profit. Obviously this is going to take some investment so let's look at the figures.

A single storey extension to create one double en-suite

Nowadays whenever we take on a new project we always maximise the properties as much as possible, and I have experience of building three single storey extensions within the last fifteen months. I can confidently say that I know I can create a 3m by 4m extension for less than £15,000. Now we know the cost and the income we can calculate the return on investment.

Income / investment = % return on investment (ROI)

En-suite rental profit / extension cost = ROI

£5,800 / £15,000 = 38.7%

This means if we invested £15,000 into an extension we would get all of our money back in just over two-and-a-half years, and then we'd make £5,800 a year more profit.

A loft conversion to create two en-suite rooms

My builder can extend into the roof and create two en-suite rooms for £20,000-£25,000. Let's assume the cost will be £25,000.

Income / investment = % ROI

Two en-suites rental profit / loft conversion cost = ROI

£11,600 / £25,000 = 46.4%

This means if we invested £25,000 into a loft extension we would get all of our money back in just under two-and-a-quarter years and then we'd make £11,600 a year more profit.

That's great I hear you say, but I don't have the £15,000 or £25,000 to spare with all these other projects I'm doing. The question is: could you afford the money in the short term? If you could invest this money for the short term, or if you could borrow it for six months, you could do the work without being out of pocket in the long term. Once you have made the developments to your property it will be worth more both in terms of its bricks and mortar value* and its commercial value**, which means you could refinance the property upon completion and should be able to get all of the money you invested back by borrowing more from the bank.

* The bricks and mortar value of a house is the amount that a non-investor would pay for the house to live in as a family home. This type of valuation does not take account of the rental income that is achieved.

** The commercial value of a property will be a multiple of the net annual rent/income that the property makes (rent - bills). Properties will generally be valued at seven to twelve times the net rent; in London properties are very sought after and would be valued commercially at twelve times rent. Properties in less desirable areas, often in the north of England, and not in or near key commercial cities, are likely to be valued closer to seven times the net annual rent. In Bristol, generally properties will be valued at nine to ten times rental income for large HMO's. Although some commercial valuers base their valuation solely on the rent achieved, more and more lenders are also comparing the property to others in the vicinity. This is because although a property may be valued commercially at a certain amount based on a formula, if the property were to be repossessed and sold at auction the buyers may not be willing to pay the higher commercial value (why would they if they could buy next door a lot cheaper?). Properties set up as HMO's are hard to value by comparing them to neighbouring properties, because only investors would buy an eight-bedroom property with six bathrooms. In this case, the valuers will often compare the property to other large HMO's in the area, and what they have sold for.

The main reason for having undeveloped properties in my portfolio is that when I started investing I had no money and wanted to acquire as many properties as quickly as I could. This was in the midst of a recession, and I really felt it was a time to be securing as many assets as possible. I knew I would always be able to develop these properties later down the line, but wouldn't always be able to secure properties at the prices and under the terms that we could then – using lease options and therefore not having to pay a deposit at the outset.

The property in the following case study was secured using a lease option contract, costing just £6,000. Even without fully developing and optimising such properties we were able to achieve an ROI of nearly 100%. I'm still not sure if this was the best decision. We were making £400-£500 a month out of these properties initially when their potential was a lot higher; if we had a bad month with a lot of maintenance we would make nothing – that doesn't really happen if you're making £1,500-£2,500 per month out of a property.

Hidden Gold Case Study: Fishponds, Bristol

When I first saw this property I knew it had massive potential. Originally it was a three-bedroom Victorian terrace but it had been extended to the side fifteen to twenty years ago to create a double garage with two extra double bedrooms above. The garage was ripe for converting into two double bedrooms with en-suites, and the loft was easily big enough to create three double bedrooms with en-suites. At the time of securing the property I was focusing on growing the portfolio rather than maximising the rent through the development.

Phase I - securing the property

This first phase was just about securing the deal and making sure the property was cash flow positive. We secured it via a lease option (please read my first book *Escape the Rat Race* to find out more about lease options). The owner of the property had moved to London with her company and had rented the property out, but there had been some hiccups with the previous tenancy and she was unsure whether to rent it or sell it. We were able to give her the best of both worlds by giving her a guaranteed rental income for up to six years and agreeing to buy it for a fair price. This meant that as well as the purchase price, she would benefit from up to six years profit (lease fee - her mortgage). We fixed the purchase price at the 2012 value of £200,000 since we would be taking full responsibility from this point. This was a great deal for us, as we would benefit in many ways:

- Rental profit of approximately £400 per month or £4,800 for the year.
- Capital growth – even if we did nothing to improve the property it was likely to increase in value over time.
- The opportunity to develop the property to massively increase the value.
- The opportunity to develop the property to benefit from increased rental income.

This was all to come later but here is how the first phase stacked up:

Our set up costs

Estate agent fee (we generally pay these when doing lease options to incentivise the owner and the agent)	£4,000
Legal fees	£800
Splitting the two reception rooms	£800
Furnishing (we got lucky with a house clearance)	£600
Total acquisition costs	**£6,200**

We agreed to pay a monthly lease fee on the property of £900. This was slightly less than market rent due to the fact that we were guaranteeing the money regardless of whether it was full or not. As part of the deal we also agreed to cover the cost of any maintenance.

Our monthly costs

Lease fee	£900
Bills	£350
Management	£130
Maintenance	£100
Total	**£1,480**

To maximise the rent without much investment we divided the reception rooms and used one of them as a bedroom, which gave us five rooms with rent of £1,850.

This gave us a monthly profit of £370 (not exactly inspiring).

The annual profit was £4,440 (again, this doesn't really set the world on fire).

Although the numbers were small, so was the investment – which meant we had a 71% ROI. That meant that we would get all our investment back in fourteen months.

Phase I cash flow

Rent	£1,850
Total monthly cost	£1,480
Cash flow	**£370**

Phase II - discovering the hidden gold

Ok, so in this example the potential cash flow wasn't exactly hidden. I knew about it from day one. I just didn't want to invest the time and money in it at the time. Now, a few years later, we're about to develop this property. We haven't got consent to do structural works so will most likely buy the property before we commence work.

Part 1 - the garage conversion

The garage is big enough to make two en-suite double rooms. Each of these would rent for £520 per month, giving a total increased rent of £1,040 per month or £12,480 per year.

Part 2 - the loft conversion

The loft is nearly twice as big as most houses because of the extension on the side. By putting a large dormer window across the entire rear side of the house it would be possible to fit three double rooms with en-suites in the loft space.

Part 3 - refurbish remaining rooms and communal areas

Whilst doing such extensive work in the rest of the house we really want to bring up the standard of the existing space. We will add en-suite bathrooms to existing bedrooms and also replace the existing kitchen. In total this would take the house from five to ten rentable rooms, all with en-suites. As this is a lot of bedrooms, we will have two kitchens and communal rooms rather than one, which means that it will effectively be a four-bedroom flat and a six-bedroom maisonette.

Schedule of works

Garage conversion	£12,000
Loft conversion	£40,000
Renovate existing house	£20,000
Furnishing	£5,000
Total	**£77,000**

Rental figures

Rent (10 x £525) (we run at 99% occupancy)	£5,250
Mortgage	£1,500
Bills	£650
Management (effectively this would be two properties)	£230
Maintenance	£200
Total monthly cost	**£2,580**

Total monthly profit	**£2,670**
Total annual profit	**£32,040**

Value increase and refinancing

Purchase price	£200,000
Cost of works	£77,000
Stamp Duty	£1,500
Solicitor	£1,000
Architect and planning	£2,000
Total cost	**£281,500**
New value	**£450,000**
Mortgage @ 70%	**£315,000**

If we are able to borrow 70% of the new value as we expect, we will get a £315,000 mortgage where the total costs are only £281,500, which means that we will not only get all of our invested funds back but will actually get £33,500 cash back out of the deal on top.

Return on investment

We have no money tied up after refinance and will make £32,040 in annual rental profit. This means the ROI is infinite!

Summary

If (like me) you have a portfolio that is not maximised you could be sitting on a goldmine. We are currently planning loft extensions on two properties and rear extensions on two other properties as well as the project in the case study in this chapter. The works that we are planning will cost £160,000 but will increase the value of the properties by £360,000. With this value increase we will be able to refinance the properties to get back everything we spend and more. In total this will increase the rental profits by over £50,000 per year, nearly twice the national average wage in this country.

It's time to review your existing portfolio. Do you have single lets that could be multi-lets? Do you have houses that could be extended into the roof or to the rear? Much of this work can be done without going through the whole planning process until May 2016 by completing the work under permitted development. Many expect this relaxation in planning legislation to be extended, at the time of writing we are still waiting to hear whether this is the case.

Chapter 9: Maximising Your Investment

"The will to win, the desire to succeed, the urge to reach your full potential … these are the keys that unlock the door to personal excellence."

Confusius

Nowadays we're fortunate enough to have the know-how to maximise every property from the outset and as we have a proven record, can attract the necessary investment. Optimising your property is one of the most important things you can do to maximise profit. If you have a five-bedroom house-share, generally speaking three rooms' rent will cover the mortgage, the fourth will cover the bills and the fifth will provide the profit. If you were able to create an extra room you could double the profit – and of course if you could create two additional rooms you would triple the profit. By maximising a property's potential it can be possible to double the rental profits. Increasing the square footage of a property and increasing the rent are also sure ways to increase the value and refinance more of your cash out of the deal through remortgaging. Maximising a property's potential is essential for anyone wanting to build a highly profitable portfolio.

Here are the top five ways to maximise the rental profits:

1. Converting a reception room into a bedroom

Some landlords convert all communal space into bedrooms to maximise the rent. This is very common in London where space is at a massive premium and rental demand is very high. In areas where demand is lower and tenants have more choice that may result in rooms being difficult to rent, you may suffer more voids and have to do more viewings to fill a room. As a landlord or business person, your time is your most valuable asset so you would have to balance maximising the profit with minimising your time invested. You may also achieve less rent with no communal space so this must be factored in when making the decision too.

Generally speaking I would suggest that one communal room is more than enough so would certainly recommend converting any additional reception rooms into bedrooms. Converting reception rooms into bedrooms is the quickest and easiest way to increase profits and it can be done at a very low cost, often just by changing the door to a fire door. So for a one-off cost of around £250 you can add £4,000-£8,000 in annual profit depending on the rents in your area. In some properties, the wall between the two reception rooms will have been removed to create open plan living space; this can easily be replaced with a stud wall for less than £1,000.

2. Dividing enormous rooms into two smaller double rooms

Bristol has a lot of large Georgian and Victorian properties. Some of the rooms within these properties can be 5m by 5m, which is twice as big as most modern double bedrooms. Although it seems a shame to divide such beautiful rooms, the numbers are too strong to ignore. A large double room will rent for up to £500 in Bristol, but we have just split one of them into two and are renting the rooms for a total of £885, a 77% uplift on the £500 we would have achieved. This is by far the simplest and cheapest way to increase the rent. It's simply a case of adding partition walls and a door. This can all be done for £1,000-£1,200, and the extra rent would pay this cost back in roughly three months.

3. Converting large bathrooms into bedrooms

The large Victorian properties that we often invest in have bathrooms of around 4m by 3m. Having a bathroom this big is not only a waste of space but can even cause problems if people spend too long in them (whilst others are waiting). Bathrooms of this size we often convert into an en-suite double room, then look to add a shower room elsewhere in the house. For a shower room you need a space of 1.3m by 1.8m.

In Bristol the extra en-suite bedroom that this will create will rent for £525, thus dramatically increasing the profit. The cost of converting a bathroom into an en-suite room will be roughly £4,000; and creating the extra shower room elsewhere will cost £2,000-£5,000 depending on the location within the house and the complexity of the plumbing. The overall cost for both the conversion of the bathroom and creating the shower room will be £7,500, and in Bristol this would generate £6,300 annual rent. This equates to an 84% ROI meaning that you would get your money back within fourteen months.

4. Extending to the rear

Although extending a property is more expensive than the other methods discussed it can still be very profitable. This is especially viable with the current relaxation of planning legislation which was brought in during the recession to try to stimulate the economy. This relaxation is in place until mid-2016 and allows you to extend 3m to the rear of the property under permitted development legislation. You can learn more about this on the government's planning portal.

We have been able to build 3m by 3m extensions for £13,000 to £17,000 as we have contacts within the trades. We use this space as a communal room and convert the existing communal room into a double en-suite bedroom. Assuming an average cost of £15,000, the increase in rent for the extra room is £6,300 for the year, which equates to a 42% ROI meaning that the investment would be paid back within two years and five months.

5. Extending into the roof

Extending into the roof is the most expensive way to create more space but this too can be profitable. Extending into the roof will cost roughly £30,000 and can also be done through the permitted development process. Assuming you can create enough space for an en-suite bedroom you will generate £6,300 rent per annum (based on our Bristol averages). This means that your ROI will be 21% meaning that it will take four years and nine months to get your investment back.

It can sometimes be possible to create two rooms within a loft conversion depending upon the size of the loft. Obviously this can make it a lot more lucrative. We have just created two en-suite rooms within a property in Bristol at a cost of £32,000. Each of the rooms is rented out for £525 per month so the total extra rent from the loft is £12,600 per annum, which equates to a 40% ROI. This means that we will get our money back within two years and six months.

Do Single Rooms Rent?

Single rooms are always harder to rent than double rooms, often attracting less interest when you advertise them and also having a lower success rate when conducting viewings. Although we always provide a communal area people tend to want their own space and often have too many belongings to fit into a single room, so the idea of being cramped up in a single room full of stuff is not appealing. Although on paper it makes sense to create as many rooms as possible, in practice it's hard work, the rooms will be vacant longer and it will take up a lot of your time. I suggest thinking carefully before dividing double rooms into singles: it may be profitable in London where space is at a premium but might not be so good elsewhere.

Increasing Value through Converting Rooms and Extending the Property

The increased rent achievable through converting rooms or extending a property is only half of the story. You will also add value to the house so this is something else to consider on top of the increased rent that you will achieve. A small single storey extension may cost £15,000 but add £25,000-£50,000 to the value of the property. A loft conversion may cost £30,000 but could add £50,000-£100,000 to the value of the house.

In Bristol, our HMO properties tend to get valued at between £45,000 and £55,000 per bedroom, depending on their location within the city and the rent that they achieve. Valuing property is not an exact science and it is not just based on the rent. This means that if all you do is change a living room into a bedroom and divide a large bedroom into two rooms, it is unlikely to increase in value by

£80,000. If done as part of a refurbishment to the whole building however, you are much more likely to get the result that you desire.

It is common to remortgage a property once you have developed it to release funds for another project. If you develop wisely you can refinance to get all of this money back.

Lease Option Case Study - Eight-Bedroom House (Five Rooms En-Suite), Harbourside, Bristol

The property - how it was

A five-bedroom Victorian terrace with beautiful views of the Harbourside in Bristol. The property consists of large rooms, many of which have great period features including a 130-year-old fireplace with marble surround, a 130-year-old wood/coal-powered cast iron stove, large 3ft ceiling roses around the lights, and beautiful cornices. The property had been rented out for a number of years and was in need of some TLC.

The location

On the waterfront in the BS8 postcode (the most desirable postcode in Bristol); just fifteen minutes' walk from the town centre and fifteen minutes' walk from Clifton centre (the posh bit). An area popular with young professionals and students alike.

The owner's situation

The property is owned outright with no mortgage in place. The owner is in his 70's and has owned the house for a number of years during which time it had become tired. He didn't particularly want to sell it but neither did he want to bring it up to a standard that would attract the best quality tenants. The property being slightly run down, the last tenants he attracted were of poor quality and caused him hassle, which was when he decided he no longer wanted to manage it. Reluctantly he put the property on the market. The owner, like the majority of people I work with, is fairly affluent, and with no mortgage he was in no urgent rush to sell. If he had any motivation, it was to get the best possible deal.

The solution

The property was on the market with a useless agent who failed to return my calls and sold the property to someone else. Two to three months later there had been no mortgage valuation by the buyer and the seller was getting frustrated. This is when he was approached by an agent that I often work with. I viewed the property and within twenty-four hours was sitting in the seller's living room with the agent discussing the best way forward.

I asked him what he was going to do with the money when he sold the property. He wasn't sure. I asked him what sort of interest he would get with that £285,000 sat in the bank. He didn't say anything, but the expression on his face demonstrated he knew it would be a pittance. I suggested that he would be able to achieve 2% return per annum in the bank and that this equated to £5,700. I explained that I would like to lease the property, and then buy it in six years for £280,000. I offered to lease it for £1,000 per month – £12,000 per annum, which is more than twice the return he would get in the bank. Being a businessman he negotiated and we settled on the following deal:

I would lease the property for up to four years.

I would pay £1,200 per month.

I would have the option to buy the property for £285,000 at any time during the lease period.

I would refurbish the property at my own cost.

I would maintain the property.

The seller was happy and later mentioned to one of my team that I was mad to give him such a good deal. From his perspective, he got a great monthly income and then got to sell at full market value.

Refurbishment

Most people investing in property using lease options want to invest as little money as possible. This quick and cheap solution was very tempting – I could have given the place a quick lick of paint and rented it for a quick profit. Instead I saw the bigger picture. This was a massive property with even bigger potential: the kind of property that you don't come across that often and the type you just know you'll want to own forever. With this in mind, and with a lot of experience in the market of renting rooms, I decided to embark upon a more extensive refurbishment, converting the bathroom to create an extra bedroom, building an extension to create another bedroom and converting one of the communal rooms into a bedroom – adding three bedrooms to make eight in total, five of them en-suite.

The numbers

Solicitor	£900
Estate agent (2%)	£5,700
Refurbishment, including extension	£28,000
HMO licence	£1,200
Total cost	**£35,800**

Monthly figures

Lease fee	£1,200
Bills	£500
Management (in-house with me doing some of the work)	£80
Total	**£1,780**
Rents	£3,350
Profit/cash flow per month	£1,570
Profit per annum	£18,840
ROI	52.6%
Current value	£375,000
Equity created through refurbishment	£90,000

This case study was written two years ago. Since then the rents have increased and the monthly profit is now £1,965 per month or £23,580 per annum and the property value is £500,000, giving us £215,000 equity.

Summary

Maximise the property to maximise the rent.

Maximise the property to maximise the value.

Convert a reception room into a bedroom.

Split very large rooms into two rooms.

Convert large bathrooms into bedrooms and find a smaller area to locate a shower room.

Extend to the rear to create an extra room.

Extend into the loft to create extra rooms.

Maximise the potential of every property.

Chapter 10: Recycle Your Cash

"I see money as a worker that I control, I continually reinvest my profits over and over again."

Warren Buffett

Investing in property is very capital intensive (bloody expensive). Typically for a £300,000 property you would need to invest:

Deposit (30% of purchase price)	£90,000
Stamp duty	£5,000
Legal fees	£1,000
Survey	£1,000
Mortgage fee	£6,000
Refurbishment	£50,000
Total investment	**£153,000**

Unless you're very wealthy already, your cash may run out quite quickly when making investments like this typical example. The safest way to invest is to pay down your mortgage as quickly as possible to reduce your debt and increase your profit. The problem is that this can be a very slow way to invest; it may be years or even decades until you're in a position to buy your next house. The faster and more popular way to invest is to buy a property, refurbish it and then refinance to borrow 70%-80% of its new increased value.

In the example above with the £300,000 property, let's imagine that post-refurbishment the property is worth £400,000. Your initial investment was £153,000, including a £90,000 deposit which means that you have a mortgage of £210,000. If the property is now worth £400,000 you should be able to borrow 75% of that valuation through remortgaging the property. Therefore you could borrow £400,000 x 75% = £300,000. In this example the bank would lend you £90,000 more than you borrowed on your original mortgage. This means that of your original £153,000 investment, you would get £90,000 back and would only have £63,000 left tied up in the property longer term. Refinancing to release £90,000 would put you in much better stead for the next investment property you want to purchase.

Getting the Best Valuation

As you can see from the example above, recycling as much of your investment as possible can really help you build a portfolio faster without running out of money. With this in mind it's obvious that the higher the valuation, the more of your cash you can recycle since you can borrow 70%-80% of the property value. So how do you ensure you get the highest valuation? With HMO's the best way to get the best valuation is to ensure the rent is as high as possible.

1. As many rooms as practical

As discussed previously in this book, the more rooms you have the more rent you'll get and therefore the higher the value of the property. This has to be done practically though; nobody wants to live in a house that feels cramped and claustrophobic, and a house like this won't impress the surveyor either.

2. En-suite bedrooms

En-suite bedrooms tend to increase rents by around 25% and will also rent out more quickly. Wherever possible include en-suite facilities within the rooms. If you are unable to go to this expense, at least ensure that there aren't too many people sharing a bathroom. The maximum number of people allowed to share a bathroom legally is five but I would aim to have no more than three or four sharing.

3. Quality workmanship

Quality workmanship will not only make your life easier as an investor (less maintenance), it will also help you to achieve the best rents. Tenants do notice when a property has been renovated well and will be willing to pay a premium. Surveyors also notice things like this and a good finish will help them to give a higher valuation.

4. Great communal space

As well as nice bedrooms it's really important to have an inviting communal space that is well equipped for the number of tenants. Ideally you want a decent-sized kitchen as well as sofas and a dining table and chairs.

5. Dressing the property

We've always been lucky in Bristol in that there is a high rental demand and therefore we haven't had to dress our properties to get them rented, so we haven't really bothered. Just recently, though, we have learnt how dressing a property can increase rents. Having trialled it for the first time I can confirm that we've been able to increase the rent by £20-£25 per room through dressing the property. It isn't expensive; it's just a case of laying the dinner table (with the crockery that you have to provide anyway), putting pictures up, making the beds, putting cushions in the rooms, etc. In larger rooms we also include small sofas to make them feel more like studios than bedrooms. Much of what you use to dress a room can be removed and used for the next property so you only need to buy the dressings once.

Summary

You want the house to feel spacious and to have a good flow. You don't want rooms that are so small that you have to squeeze past the bed to get to the wardrobe, etc. You want to create a space that the tenants will be happy to live in – they will complain less and stay longer, and you will also get better rents for a more spacious house. Most importantly, you want to create a great place to live because it's the right thing to do. Although we generally have seven- to eight-bedroom properties to create the most profit, we regularly get feedback that the houses don't feel small or cramped; they actually feel spacious and airy.

Chapter 11:
Dealing With Risk

"*Risk comes from not knowing what you're doing.*"

Warren Buffett

Assessing the Risk

When working on bigger property deals it's not just the profits that increase; the losses can also increase. This is why it's so important to assess the risks. Contrary to popular belief, entrepreneurs, business people and investors are actually very risk adverse. It's not that they don't do the deals because of risk, it's more a case that they assess and then mitigate the risks.

There are two things to consider when assessing risks: the *severity* of the risk and also the *probability* of it occurring. There are some risks that would be very severe but very unlikely to happen – for example the bank manager decides he doesn't like you and feeds all your money, including your refurbishment fund, to his pet pig. That would be very severe but very unlikely; therefore it shouldn't stop you doing the project. A good idea would be to list the risks and then score them in terms of severity and probability.

Using the silly example above – bank manager feeds your money to his pet pig:

Severity 5 out of 5

Probability 0 out of 5

You can then combine the probability and severity to give you a score:

Severity x Probability = Risk

5 x 0 = 0 out of 25

Looking at the other extreme, let's say you have to complete the building, a twenty-five-bedroom house, starting from scratch, in a week or you lose all of your money:

Severity 5 out of 5

Probability 5 out of 5

5 x 5 = 25. Maximum – it's going to happen and it's going to wipe you out – don't do the deal.

Let's now look at some more realistic examples.

- You need to get planning permission or the project won't make any money.

  Severity 4 out of 5

  Probability 3 out of 5

  4 x 3 = 12. This is quite a significant risk. Ideally you would want to eliminate this risk or mitigate it. I will work through this later.

- Another quick example: you will run over budget, run out of money and not be able to complete the project.

Severity 5 out of 5

Probability 3 out of 5

3 x 5 = 15. Again this is a significant risk that will need to be dealt with.

Mitigating Risk

After assessing the risk in terms severity and probability, the next step of the process is to reduce the chance of it happening as much as possible and also to take steps to lessen the severity/impact if it does happen. The key element of mitigating risk is to have the right people around you with the right knowledge and experience. There will be problems that you could never foresee unless you've been through the process of doing a large project.

Elimination

The best thing you can do with risk is to eliminate it wherever possible. In the example of the risk of not getting planning permission, agreeing with the seller to buy subject to you getting planning permission would eliminate the risk completely. In this case the only thing you will be risking is the money that you need to spend to apply for planning permission. Of course you may be able to achieve a better price if you buy the property without the planning but you do so at a much higher risk. It's better to make a smaller profit with no risk than taking on a high risk for a larger profit.

If you are to agree a price subject to getting planning permission, it is imperative that you secure your deal before you go through the process. The last thing you want to do is to agree a deal, go through the planning process and then have the seller pull out and sell the property to someone else for more money due to all your hard work.

You can secure your interest in the property either by signing a legally binding option contract that the seller cannot back out of, or you can exchange contracts on the purchase of the property subject to getting planning permission. These are two simple ways of achieving the same aim. You should be aware that if the planning permission goes through and you have exchanged you would be obliged to buy the property. In this case you will need to have your finances lined up ready to buy because usually you would need to complete the transaction quickly.

Reducing the Risk

If you are not able to buy subject to getting planning permission the risk can be reduced by carrying out research to fully understand the situation. For example, if the risk was that you might not get planning permission for your proposed development, you would be very wise to check through the local planning policies. Obviously if there seemed a low chance of getting approval you would be crazy to go ahead.

You also have the option of doing a pre-application enquiry, which is a lot cheaper than a full planning application and will take six weeks rather than three to four months. A seller is more likely to be willing to wait six rather than sixteen weeks.

If the seller is unwilling to wait for you to get planning permission or even a pre-planning application there are still other ways to mitigate the risk. If, after reading the local planning policies, you feel you have a good chance of getting permission you can increase your chance of doing so by including in your planning application all of the aspects of your development that are in line with the policy, and how your development will benefit the local community.

This will maximise your chance of getting planning approval and therefore minimise probability of the risk.

The other key way to minimise a risk is by reducing the severity of the risk if it does occur. In the example of the risk of not getting planning permission, for example, having a plan B ready in case planning is refused would minimise the severity of the risk. Let's say you wanted to turn an office block into a residential HMO and needed planning, could you devise a plan B that would still make a profit even if it's not your preferred solution? Having a plan C to add to this would be even better. Plans B and C may not be ideal but there is nothing worse than losing money on a project that you have spent time and money on. So in the example above, if you weren't allowed to convert to an HMO, maybe as a plan B you could convert to flats? If you couldn't do that, is there a profitable use for the building that wouldn't require any planning permission at all?

Another example of a risk may be that of running out of money before the project is complete. If this happens the property could be repossessed and you would lose a lot, or perhaps all, of your money.

These are just two examples of risks that you can eliminate or mitigate. When considering a project it is a really good idea to brainstorm all of the risks that you are facing and then go through the process of assessing all of them in terms of severity and probability, ideally trying to eliminate each risk or, if that is not possible, minimising both the probability and the severity.

Quick List of Potential Risks

House burning down

Not getting the planning permission you require

Running out of money

Not being able to sell the property at the end

Not being able to rent the property

Running out of time (loan periods from bridging companies and investors may only be for a few months).

These are just a few of the risks you may face. Take time to assess all the risks of any project you wish to take on, and discuss them with your mentor or peer group of other investors or business people.

Don't Bet Everything You Have on a Deal

As exciting as big deals are, it's not wise to bet everything you have on one deal. No deal is worth losing your home or the rest of your portfolio over. There will always be other deals!

Always Have a Buffer

Things will always go wrong. I know this sounds a bit negative but it's a fact and if you keep this in mind you can set your business up so that when things do go wrong they are a blip, not a catastrophe. If you haven't got money, even the smallest problems can become big problems. Trust me, I ran a business this way for the first two or three years. If a fridge broke in one of the houses at the end of the month before the rents came in, that would often be a big problem for us. If a boiler died in one of the houses, it would have been a catastrophe – no matter what time of the month it was. A lot of this was down to my refusal to get a job after I was sacked. My stubbornness was useful for keeping me going when times were really hard but it also made my life difficult when money was tight. Having a reliable income stream whilst building a portfolio is a really good idea; if you're determined to go full time in property then it is essential you have a buffer or at the very least some available credit on a credit card. That will give you great peace of mind.

Insuring Your Property

Whilst on the subject of risk, I can't stress highly enough the importance of making sure you are fully insured. Over the last few years some very good friends of mine have lost a lot of money because they weren't properly insured. One friend had a house burn down and later found out he wasn't insured to cover this for some reason (I don't remember the details). Another friend had a large development of three high-end flats burgled just as they were completed; the thieves took everything because they could tell that the property was vacant, including the heating systems, the bathroom suites, the wiring, even the tiles off the roof. This cost her tens of thousands of pounds because her JV partner's office manager had accidentally bought standard insurance which didn't cover properties that are vacant whilst being refurbished. Vacant properties, especially those being refurbished, are a prime target for criminals because they know nobody is living there, and they know they will be able to access brand new boilers, bathroom suites, even the plumbing and wiring which is very valuable.

When insuring a property, it is essential to tell the insurance company or broker exactly what you will be doing with the property and especially whether it will be vacant and for how long. Putting this to them in writing should ensure that you are fully protected and that they can't try to wriggle out of paying.

Perceived Risk vs. Actual Risk

Many people avoid larger properties because they feel they might be harder work and higher risk. It's logical to think there will be more hassle and more risk with an eight-bedroom property compared to a five-bed. More tenants to deal with, more wear and tear, more chance of hassle between the tenants. None of the above is as significant as you may think: there may be some increased wear and tear but in the scheme of things it is quite insignificant. As for arguments between tenants, we don't necessarily get more complaints in larger houses than in smaller ones; the dynamics seem to be different in larger houses. I think it would be worse to live in a small house with someone you don't get on with than in a large one. I can't speak from first-hand experience as I don't have anything to do with the tenants so I can only go by what is reported back to me by our lettings manager.

As for the risk of dealing with larger houses, I find these a lot less risky than smaller ones. If you rely on a single tenant to pay your mortgage and they don't pay or they leave, how will you cover the mortgage payments? You would have to find the money yourself if you can afford to, otherwise you risk losing the house. Also in a small house where you make £100-£200 profit per month (which is typical for a single let property), what do you do if the boiler breaks and the replacement is £1,500? Hopefully you'll have the funds to replace it but even so, that would wipe out the whole year's profit. Are smaller houses starting to feel a bit risky?

With a five-bedroom house-share typically the rent from three rooms will cover the mortgage, the fourth room will cover the bills and the fifth would provide the profit. In this scenario if a tenant doesn't pay or moves out, that wipes out your profit – which is far from ideal but at least all of your costs are covered. Investing in larger properties is not only a great way to spread the risk but to actually reduce it.

Looking at an eight-bedroom house generally, three to four rooms would pay the mortgage, one would cover the utility bills, leaving three rooms all providing profit. In this example you only need five out of the eight rooms to be rented to cover your costs. Depending on where you live, the rent for three rooms will be between £1,000 and £2,000 per month. With this kind of profit you can deal with any bumps in the road. Last year we had a boiler fail in an eight-bedroom property, but it is so profitable that we paid for the boiler and still made a profit that month. If this had been a single let the boiler failure would have wiped out the profit for the whole year.

Renting a house to a single tenant is generally thought to be the most simple and low risk. This is similar to most people's view about how safe and secure a good job is compared to running a business or making money through investments. I used to have the same view until I was sacked! Then I realised just how risky it is to have all of your income coming in from one source, as within minutes I was sacked and the illusion was smashed. You can read more about that story in my first book *Escape the Rat Race*.

My wife recently explained why she started investing in property. She had just graduated and started a job with Dixons as a graduate trainee. Within the first few months of starting work there, people who had worked for the company all of their lives were being called into offices and leaving in tears. They were being made redundant. These people had families who were all reliant on this sole income. Rupinder said she decided at that moment that she never wanted to be in that position and bought her first house soon afterwards.

Summary

- Brainstorm all of the risks into a list.
- Assess each risk in terms of severity.
- Assess each risk in terms of probability.
- Calculate the score for each risk.
- Wherever possible eliminate the risk.
- Mitigate remaining risks by reducing the chance of them occurring.
- Mitigate risks by decreasing their impact/severity if they do occur.
- As well as a plan A, also have a plan B and ideally a plan C.
- Fully and appropriately insure your property.

Chapter 12:
Creating A Support Network

"You are the average of the five people you spend the most time with."

Jim Rohn

Building a Great Power Team

As you get more properties under your belt and start to focus on bigger deals you'll soon realise that you can't do it on your own. If you do try and do it all on your own you'll most likely make yourself miserable doing jobs that you don't enjoy, that you are no good at, and that you could often get done for £10-£20 per hour. For your own sanity I urge you to start building a power team. Having the right team in place can make you a fortune; just this week my accountant saved me £25,000 in VAT by instructing the builders to only charge me 5% VAT on a conversion rather than the standard 20%, and provided the paperwork to justify this. So I will save 15% x £170,000 = £25,500. The cost of this service was £720 for a few hours of the guy's time. That's a great ROI and just one of the ways a good accountant can save you money on tax. So who do you need on your power team and how much will it cost? Let's start at the beginning:

Good estate agents

The first thing you need to do is to find the deal, therefore you will want to build up good relationships with estate agents. You don't need to pay these guys; the seller pays them to sell the property and it's illegal for them to take money from you when the seller is paying them to represent their best interests.

You get estate agents on board by doing what you say you're going to do. This starts with being on time for the viewing, and also by getting back to them promptly and demonstrating that you can get the purchase done quickly. As I'm more experienced now I will calculate my costs before viewing the property so that I know what I can afford to pay. I remember this figure and then the viewing is just a case of checking that everything is as expected; if there is anything unforeseen I can adjust my offer accordingly. On the last two properties I bought I took proof of funds to the viewing to prove I could buy the properties for cash, and made the offers then and there. This is a very simple but powerful way to let estate agents know that you are serious.

A good solicitor

You will need to act quickly to ensure you don't lose the deal to another investor. Your solicitor is key to this so you need to instruct them as soon as the offer is accepted. A good solicitor will be fast but thorough and will not delay the sale. They should also specialise in the type of deals you are doing. Good solicitors are often busy so it is your responsibility to keep on top of things and push them along where necessary.

A good broker

Buying cash is the simplest and fastest way to buy property but unfortunately this is not always possible. If you are buying with a mortgage or a bridging loan you will need a broker to get you the best deal available in the quickest possible time. Commercial mortgages often take three months to process so it is essential that your broker is on the ball to make sure that you don't lose the deal.

A good planning consultant

If you are looking at large developments you really need a good planning consultant. Getting the desired planning will make you a fortune and larger developments can be more technical, so don't try to scrimp here by doing the application yourself. The planning consultant we recently used was previously the head of planning in the council so she knew exactly how to put the application forward in the correct way. After a two-month delay (the council were short-staffed) we got the exact permission that we wanted for four flats with nineteen bedrooms.

A good architect

A good architect will be able to help you design your project and get the best use of space. In our big project initially there were only twelve en-suites out of nineteen rooms, but through the consultation we were able to reconfigure parts of the design to get en-suites in all nineteen bedrooms. From a cash flow perspective, this gave us £100 extra rent per room per month, adding £8,400 to the rent and therefore profit. This increase in rent in turn increased the value of the property by £80,000. A good architect will also help to present the development in the best light to the planning department.

A good builder

It's essential to have a builder to ensure you get the project done to the right standard, on time, and at the right price. Builders should be able to head up small- to medium-sized projects and call in the necessary tradespeople as required.

A good project manager

Some jobs are too big for your average builder. Generally, if there is a big conversion of an office block into multiple residential units I suggest you use a project manager to oversee the site. Although there is an extra cost involved you can still save money if the project manager can get the job done quickly. You have to weigh up the cost of the project manager against the cost of delays. Delays are often more expensive if you count the high cost of bridging that you pay during those delays and also the lost rent caused by the delay. The rent on our biggest project is over £10,000, so every month's delay costs us £10,000.

A good lettings manager

Once your project is complete it's down to your lettings manager or lettings agent to fill the property as quickly as possible with the best tenants at a good rental price. On an ongoing basis, the lettings manager's role is to be the face of the business as far as tenants are concerned. They will deal with any problems that the tenant may have and ensure the rents come in on time. A well-trained lettings manager will be able to do this on their own, except for perhaps five to ten questions a week that they will need to escalate to you, even if they are managing a sizeable portfolio. If you don't have a good manager in place you will end up spending large parts of the day dealing with tenant issues making it hard to focus on building the portfolio (which you should be doing).

A good lettings manager should also be able to liaise with the maintenance staff to deal with day-to-day issues. It is down to you to choose whether you employ somebody to work for you or use a lettings agent. Employing somebody directly can initially take a lot of effort with the training involved, but if you plan on building a large portfolio it can help you in the long run. One of the benefits of employing someone is that you pay a wage rather than a fee. We pay a staff member an hourly rate rather than an agent's percentage fee that includes the agency's profit; an agent (in our area) would charge 10% of the rent. Agents also charge landlords fees for setting up new tenancies, which is another cost that can add up to a lot of money. If you cover this process 'in-house' you can charge the tenants a fee that will cover some of the cost of employing your own lettings manager.

A good maintenance guy (or girl)

It's really important to keep your tenants happy and your properties in good condition, as it makes them easy to rent at high rental levels while also helping to maintain the value of the property. To achieve this, you need to have one or two maintenance staff with a wide range of basic 'handyman' skills. You don't necessarily need to employ these people – you can use contractors – but it is important that you are able to rely on them.

In addition, you will also need access to multiple trades to cover skilled work, such gas safe engineers and electricians for periodic safety checks.

A good accountant

A good accountant can save you a fortune in tax in perfectly legal and legitimate ways. The £25,500 VAT that mine has just saved me is just one example. There are other significant tax avoidance strategies, such as buying properties through companies, claiming capital allowances against the plant and machinery within HMO's, which can be offset against your income tax bill, reducing it to nothing. Accountants are the reason that wealthy people avoid taxes, so if you want to be wealthy your accountant is a key part of your power team.

Contracts

Substantial amounts of work that you get someone to do should be covered by a contract. This will not only protect both parties but will also clearly establish what is expected from each party at the outset. I have learnt the hard way that you cannot simply rely on trust; you leave yourself too vulnerable.

Getting a mentor

With all the information available on the internet, is it really essential to have a mentor?

There is a lot of free information online, but that information tends to conflict and it's hard to know who to believe. I listened to a webinar recently where the presenter said that en-suites were a hassle and that rent-wise it wasn't really worth it. He went on to admit that he had never actually let any en-suite rooms, but the few tenants he had asked had said they weren't really bothered about them and would prefer a slightly bigger room instead. We have 140 rooms (mainly ours but a few managed for others), and out of that 140, 114 have en-suites. The average rent for an en-suite is just under £100 more than a double room. If we had listened to the 'expert' on the internet, the rooms would make £11,400 less profit per month. That's £136,800 less profit per year! Since HMO's are valued based on rent, our portfolio (plus the few that we manage) would be worth **£1.37 million** less without the en-suites.

With so much information available, you need to be very selective about what advice you take. The alternatives are to test things out yourself or to get a mentor with the relevant experience. You could, for example, buy a six-bedroom house, convert three to en-suite rooms, have one bathroom for the other three rooms to share, and test what rents you can achieve – the problem is that half of the rooms won't be as profitable, therefore the house will also be less valuable, and you will leave tens of thousands of pounds in the deal. This is just a simple example of a mistake that would cost a lot more than getting expert advice. In my opinion, getting a mentor is a must. I have used mentors throughout my property career and have received great benefit from them.

The best way to move forward quickly is to get a mentor. A mentor will not only move you forward faster but also help you avoid all the mistakes that they made whilst they were learning. The cost of mistakes is considerable and when working on bigger deals everything is amplified, including the cost of the mistakes. You need to decide – do you want to spend your money on a mentor or on mistakes? Generally mistakes are the more expensive and most painful option.

A good mentor will also have contacts that you can take advantage of to help you build that essential power team that every great investor needs. A good mentor's experience can be so valuable that a single comment or contact can make (or save) you thousands of pounds. When you work with a mentor, you are buying their five, ten or even twenty years of experience rather than their hours of time.

The only question is who should you choose as a mentor? Here are the things that I think you should consider when searching for the right person:

Do you like them?

Personally I think it's really important that you like and respect your mentor. You will be spending valuable time with them and it's important that you get on.

Are your values in alignment?

Values are very important. I really value honesty and integrity. To give you an example, I'm naturally an introvert and could really use some help in promoting my training business when speaking on stage. I went to see probably the best person in the UK in terms of selling from the stage. I watched his presentation and then saw one hundred people running to sign up to his £5,000 course. He made £500,000 worth of sales in less than an hour – but I wasn't one of them. Why? Because he wasn't honest and ethical in the way that he sold. I would prefer to make tens of thousands of pounds less each year than sell in a dishonest and unethical way.

Do they inspire you?

There may be a lot of tough times on your property journey, including many rejections and knock-backs. Choose a mentor who will encourage you to keep going when times are hard and who will help you to keep your eye on the goal – your dream life.

Do you trust them?

If you don't trust your mentor it will be almost impossible to get the most out of them. You'll end up analysing everything they tell you to do rather than just getting on with it. That will cost you a lot of time and money. You may not agree with everything they say but you have to trust them.

Have they achieved what you want to achieve?

The right mentor will have achieved what you want to achieve in whatever area of business the mentoring is in. The idea is that you can benefit from your mentor's successes and failures without having to experience the same failures yourself. If your mentor does not have the relevant experience, they're not the best person for you.

Can they teach as well as do?

It's really important that your mentor can teach as well as do the deals. Some of the best people in any business cannot put things into the simplest terms so that they are easy to understand. A good mentor should be able to simplify things, and then explain in a different way if you don't understand.

Will they stretch your thinking?

You really need someone who will stretch your thinking through both their questions and their actions. A good mentor will ask great questions, but also stretch your thinking through their own actions and investments; ideally your mentor will be doing great deals themselves and will act as an example for you to follow.

Are they just in it for the money?

Unfortunately, as in any industry, some people are just in the property training and mentoring business for the money. It's really important that you choose a mentor who really cares about your results. If it's all about the money for them, you won't get the best out of them. When considering a mentor make sure you ask as many people as possible about them to find out if they're in it for the right reasons.

Summary

Property and pretty much all businesses are team sports, and your job is to create the winning team. I excel in very few things in property so I play to my strengths and build a team to do the rest. Within our property business I'm great at creating deals, negotiating, maximising a property's potential and leading the team based on the vision we hold. I also promote the business to investors but that's about as far as my expertise can stretch. I'm useless at viewings; if I ever have to do them I pretty much open the door, point to the room and say, "*This is the room …*". I shrug, and then there's a long silence! I'm not good at small talk with the tenants but I don't need to be. Over 90% of the tenants I haven't even met, but it doesn't matter: our occupancy rates are 99% and non-payments or late payments virtually zero. Just focus on your strengths and build a great team around you. You'll be a lot happier and a lot richer as a result.

Chapter 13:
Financing Deals - Mortgages And Bridging Loans

"If you owe the bank $100 that's your problem. If you owe the bank $100 million, that's the bank's problem."

J. Paul Getty

Mortgages - is Interest Only Best or Should You be Paying Down the Capital too?

Many property investment seminars tell you to use interest only mortgages to maximise your cash flow. If you take out an interest only mortgage then you will not be paying a big chunk off the capital every month, so will have more available cash to play with. Looking at the numbers it's very easy to argue that you should purely use interest only mortgages, and use the capital raised to reinvest in new projects. Doing this would allow you to reinvest your profits into new ventures and therefore maximise your returns by using the compound effect.

Albert Einstein said that compound interest is the eighth wonder of the world. He who understands it earns it, and he who doesn't pays it. So what is the compound effect and how does it work? Compounding means continually reinvesting your profit so that you not only get a return on your investment, but you also get a return on the reinvested profits. Let's say you invest £100,000 and get an annual return of 10%, by the end of the year you have £110,000; if you then invest this £110,000 and again get a rate of 10% by the end of year two you would have £121,000; if you reinvest all of this, at the end of twenty-four years the £100,000 investment would be worth £1 million. Generally in property, if you buy high cash-flowing HMO's it should be possible to achieve a 20%+ return on the cash you invest so you could get to a million in just thirteen years if you continually reinvest the profits.

With property you not only get the great cash flow, you also get capital growth over the long term. If you buy a house, again generally speaking, it will be worth twice as much in ten to fifteen years. With this additional bonus there is a strong argument to say that you should not only choose interest only and invest all of your cash returns into more property ventures, but that you should also constantly remortgage the portfolio to make more funds available to reinvest. This would allow you to take advantage of both the cash returns and the equity within the portfolio, effectively allowing you to get the maximum leverage and maximum compound effect. It almost sounds good to be true, doesn't it? But the numbers can't be argued with – they're based on basic mathematic principles. The theory is flawless, the numbers are 100% correct … but there is one problem – the numbers and the theory are based on everything going smoothly. Anyone who has been in property or in any other business will know that generally things don't always go smoothly. The financial sums fail to take one critical thing into account – risk! If you continually use interest only mortgages and refinance to withdraw as much cash as possible you leave yourself wide open to risks. What would you do if interest rates soared and wiped out all the profits or even turned your cash flow/profits into losses? What if the property market crashed by 30% like it did in 2008/2009? If you have only 25% equity in each property, this would put you into negative equity. At this point the banks could call in your loans and take away the portfolio that you have worked so hard to build up. That might be extreme but if you read your mortgage terms most would say that you need to maintain the 25% equity you have in the property even if prices go down, so it is possible.

My aim is not to scare you away from investing – investing can make you very wealthy – my goal is to help you hold on to the wealth you create. How you choose to invest will depend on your risk profile and this can vary over time depending on where you are in your investment journey. When I started investing in property I was sacked, broke and had nothing to lose. At this point my risk tolerance was very high: to survive and avoid having to go back with my tail between my legs and try to get another job I had to build cash flow very quickly, and would have done anything ethical to increase my cash flow. I didn't consider in detail how risky any of the investments were; I didn't ponder too long about what would happen if the market crashed or if interest rates soared; my main risk at the time was running out of money for basic necessities such as food and shelter. Fortunately I got through that phase even though sometimes things went very wrong. Through all of the trials and tribulations, I built up a multi-million pound property portfolio with over a million pounds of equity.

Now I have a new problem – I have something to lose. As you can imagine, as my wealth changed so did my attitude to risk – especially having experienced some fairly substantial losses on my journey. Having seen many ups and downs in the property market (and regularly taken advantage of them) I want to ensure that I protect myself against this volatility. I want to ensure that I remain wealthy. This doesn't mean that I'm not continuing to grow my portfolio, it just means that I'm protecting against the downside. Now I have more cash flow than I need so when I buy a new property I don't need to squeeze every last penny out of it in terms of monthly cash flow. Rather than making £2,000 a month out of a property, I'm more than happy to take a repayment mortgage which will give me £1,500 in my pocket every month and pay down the mortgage by £500-£600 every month – in a year that's £6,000-£7,000 paid off the mortgage. Now, when I look at various mortgage products I take a more balanced view – do I want to pay 5.5% on an interest only mortgage, or less than 4% with a repayment? Personally I would prefer to take the sub-4% option. On a £200,000 mortgage, the 1.5% reduction in the rate means that the interest is £3,000 less per year – that money is better in my pocket than in the bank's. Taking this option reduces the interest by £250 per month so even though I am paying £600 off of the capital every month, the mortgage is only £350 more expensive than the interest only equivalent.

Fixed Rate or Variable Rate

Another key question when considering what mortgage to take is whether to go for a variable interest rate or a fixed interest rate. Interest rates are low at the time of writing (2015) and don't look as if they will change drastically anytime soon. Currently it's possible to get sub 4% rates on commercial mortgages, which is very low – commercial mortgages are often over 6% because they are more specialist than normal buy-to-let mortgages. Mortgage rates under 4% are very tempting, especially when rates seem like they will be low for quite a while. It's easy to see why these are popular with lots of investors. Why would somebody choose a fixed mortgage when rates are so low? With the current low rates and anticipated continuation of these, a number of long term fixed rate mortgage products are also available. We recently agreed a rate of 4.99% fixed for ten years. In the short to medium term we are paying an extra 1% per annum on a £250,000 mortgage, which is an extra £2,500 per year (£208 per month). Although I'd love to have the extra £208 per month in the short term, the long term stability is well worth the cost. Since this is a repayment mortgage the rate is still less than the interest only mortgages currently available, and it's fixed for ten years. Although rates are currently at all-time lows things will not stay this way and if inflation increases, interest rates will be sure to increase too. Within this ten years we will have paid £90,000 off the mortgage, which is a great feeling.

What you choose to do with your mortgage will depend upon your risk profile but I certainly think long term fixed rates are good for long term wealth and security. Maybe you don't want to pay the higher fixed rates on all of your mortgages but it would be wise to hedge the risk with some of them. There are some mortgage rates available where you can fix part of the mortgage and have the other portion of the mortgage on a variable rate, and you can choose whether to fix 10% of the mortgage or 90%, depending on your risk profile.

Bridging - is it Too Expensive?

Many people are scared of bridging; they often know of somebody who had to take out a bridging loan at some point and had to pay extortionate fees. Is bridging really that bad? Is it something to be avoided at all costs? Bridging can be very expensive – you will often have to pay a 2% set up fee, a £1,000 survey fee and often £1,000 for the bridging company's legal fees as well as a similar figure to cover your own legal fees. Then you can expect to pay 1%-1.5% per month in interest, that's 12%-18% per year. These costs really add up. Even if you only need to take a bridging loan for one month it's likely to cost you in excess of £10,000 on a reasonable-sized property.

Bridging loans are not ideal but that doesn't mean that you should avoid bridging completely. Some of the best deals are not possible to do using standard mortgages, either because you need to buy quickly (and commercial mortgages often take three months to acquire) or because the property is not mortgageable. Some deals are great and will allow you to refurbish and then remortgage at a much higher value and get all of your investment back, leaving you with no cash tied up in the deal long term. It is definitely worth taking out bridging loans for these deals.

Interest Risk and Stress Testing

When considering a variable rate mortgage, it is essential that you consider what the mortgage might cost you when interest rates increase. Commercial lenders often charge 4%-5% above the Bank of England base rate. At the time of writing interest rates are 0.5%, which is the lowest they have ever been. This means that you can currently get commercial mortgages at around 4%-6% on a variable rate. This is great and can allow you to make a good profit in the short term but you must check what the mortgage would cost you if interest rates increased. If the Bank of England increased the base rate to 5% and you are paying 4% above the base rate, you will have to pay 9% interest. That would double the cost of your monthly payments and could wipe out your profits. This is why it's essential to calculate the effect interest rates will have on your mortgage payments before you buy the house.

Summary

Choosing your mortgage products will depend on where you are within your property journey. At first you may want to choose interest only mortgages to maximise your cash flow and reach your financial freedom figure. Once you're financially free it's a great idea to choose some repayment mortgages to reduce your debt over the years. In the long term, interest rate rises pose one of the biggest risks to investors so it's a good idea to try to fix rates for the long term where possible.

When considering a bridging loan make sure the deal is great so that you can justify the high cost of borrowing. The more cautious among you will balk at the eye-watering finance costs but you need to compare the cost of borrowing with the cost of losing the deal. It's worth paying a few grand a month interest for a few months if the deal will make you a few grand a month forever.

Chapter 14: Attracting Funding For Your Deals

"The first rule is not to lose. The second rule is not to forget the first rule."

Warren Buffett

Let's face it, even investors with the deepest pockets might run out of investment capital at some stage. The traditional way to grow a portfolio is to save up your income from your job, save the rental profits, wait a few years and then invest when you have enough money in the bank. This is certainly the most secure way to invest and it will make you very wealthy eventually, as it has for many others. The problem with this method is the 'eventually' part of the equation – we've just come out of the largest recession the world has ever seen and properties look certain to rise steadily over the next few years. Do you want to wait three to five years to buy the next property knowing that it may be 20%-50% more expensive by the time you buy it? I thought not.

There is another way. It is a more risky way to invest so if you choose to proceed along this route you must do so with caution. This route of course is to invest with other people's money. There are generally two ways of doing this: you can either borrow money from others to invest, or you can invest on a joint venture (JV) basis.

Borrowing to Invest

After using your own funds, the next simplest way to invest is probably by borrowing somebody else's money as it is very clear what each party's responsibilities are. One party lends a set amount of money for a set period of time for a set interest rate. This is very clear and easy to understand. The money can be borrowed from banks or from individuals. You will need to check with the mortgage provider whether this is acceptable and under what terms you are allowed to do it. Many banks will only allow you to invest with money given to you by direct family members such as husbands, wives, mothers, fathers or siblings. If you wish to borrow money from anyone else you will need to do so before you run out of money; this way you can prove to the bank that you have the deposit. You then buy the property, and subsequently borrow the funds to replace your savings. It is possible to repeat this process several times. It may, however, not be in line with your mortgage company's terms and conditions and it is down to you to check that out.

This method of investing can be extremely risky. You are effectively taking out 100% borrowing against the property (25%-30% from the investor and 70%-75% from the bank). Before the global economic crisis, banks would lend 100% finance to buy houses, but the outcome was that many of the borrowers were forced to go bankrupt and the lenders lost an absolute fortune, some of them, such as Northern Rock, ending up insolvent.

If you are considering this method of investing you have a duty to your investors to be very careful with their money. You must assess the risks in even more detail than you would if it was your own money. You must eliminate as many of the risks as possible and where risks cannot be eliminated completely, you must mitigate them. You must have a crystal clear strategy and a crystal clear method of repaying the money within the specified time. You must also have a Plan B: things can and will go wrong, so how will you repay the person if things don't turn out as planned? In the worst case scenario, do you have other assets that can be sold to repay the debt? All of these things need to be thought through and discussed with the lender when agreeing the loan. It may feel that highlighting the potential pitfalls will scare off the investor but personally I have found that people really appreciate the open and honest approach and will respect and trust you more for treating them this way.

If your intentions are good you should have no qualms in offering the lender a second legal charge against one of your properties to give them security. At the very least you should offer them a restriction against the title of one of your properties, if not the property that you are using their money to buy.

There are risks with every deal and although these can be reduced I need to point out that basing your whole strategy around borrowing from other people multiplies the risks not just for you, but for the people lending you money. Solely investing this way is like building a tower of cards; if one deal/card falters your whole portfolio can come crashing down, you could face bankruptcy and the investors/lenders would lose a lot of money.

So When is it Right to Borrow Money to Invest?

Clearly there are risks to investing with other people's money but there is also a very positive side to this too. I have bought many properties by borrowing funds from private individuals, and have given them an interest rate four to five times higher than the miserable rates that the banks will give them. So when is it good to borrow money from others? In my opinion you should only borrow in this way to do exceptionally good deals; the deal should be so good that you can easily pay the investor back on time, with the agreed interest, and still make a great profit whilst doing so. You should never do high risk deals with other people's money, and you shouldn't do deals that have to run perfectly smoothly to be able to pay the person back.

Creating Joint Venture Partnerships to Invest

It is also possible to work with investors on a JV basis where both the risk and the rewards are shared. There are many ways to put these deals together and to split roles and responsibilities. The way that I use JV's is that I source the property, manage the purchase, manage the refurbishment and my team manage the property on an ongoing basis. If the JV partner wishes to learn about property investing I will use the deal and other deals that I'm doing at the time to teach them how to invest. The JV partner simply puts in the money for the deposit, the legal and financing costs, and the refurbishment. Sometimes the investor takes on the mortgage depending on how involved they wish to be; taking on the mortgage will help them build a relationship and reputation with the bank and make it easier for them to invest in future if they wish to do so. Other times we take on the mortgage ourselves, as this helps us to get the best mortgages because we have a wide range of experience and a great track record. Both the profit and the risk is shared on a 50:50 basis in terms of the equity and the rental profit (equity is only shared once the investor has been repaid, usually through refinancing or through selling). If a loss were to be made in terms of equity or a rental loss, both parties would have to pay for the loss equally.

For the partner who finds the deal, the JV structure is generally one where they will make less profit than if they were to invest with borrowed funds, but there would also likely be less risk. When you invest with a JV partner, the JV partner usually gets their funds back when the property can be refinanced. With really good deals, all the funds can be refinanced through remortgaging the property after it has been refurbished, but you need to add significant value to be able to do this. Often you will need to refinance after refurbishment to get around half of the investor's funds out, and then refinance the property again in three to five years to return the rest. Because it is the property that owes the investor the money rather than you, there is less pressure. With loans, you must return the funds by a certain date whether the deal goes to plan or not. There are lots of ups and downs with property so joint venturing on some deals, sharing the risk and reward, is a prudent strategy.

Borrowing to invest or joint venturing enables people to build a portfolio without investing any money. Some property investors will want to do as many of these deals as possible to quickly build a portfolio. I urge you not to do this. You owe it to the financial investors to be careful with their money. I have occasionally thought that I should lower my criteria for property so that I can find more deals and build a portfolio more quickly, but have always snapped out of this train of thought quite quickly. I only do deals with investors that I would do myself with my own money. It's just not ethical to treat other people's money with less respect than your own. Quality is always better than quantity. It's much better to own five properties that make £2,000 a month each rather than ten properties that make £1,000 each. Building a portfolio on small margins is a false economy. It's hard work – believe me, I've tried it. Some of my first deals only made £300-£400 profit per month, which meant that if there were any problems with the property we wouldn't make any money and would even make a loss some months. We quickly learnt a lesson and set a rule of not taking a property on if it made less than £500 per month. Since then we've moved this up to a minimum of £1,000 per month and more recently

£1,500 per month after all costs. Soon this figure will be moving to £2,000 per month.

Steps to Ensure You're Building a Robust Portfolio

Minimise the amount of money you borrow as much as possible.

Always have an exit strategy, ideally more than one.

Plan for things to go wrong but to still succeed.

Always have a Plan B.

Ensure lenders/investors are aware of the risks.

Discuss with lenders ways to minimise the risks.

Marketing for Joint Venture Partners

There are strict laws about marketing for JV partners. It is illegal to market JV's to the general public. This was made illegal to try to prevent the public being ripped off. Con men have regularly sold worthless investments to vulnerable people who don't understand them, and the government has rightfully taken steps to eradicate this.

It is legal to actively offer investments to close friends, family, sophisticated investors and high net worth individuals. If people approach you wanting to invest in your ventures, then it is ok to deal with them but it would be wise to get them to sign disclaimers stating that they have approached you wanting to invest, and not the other way round.

Why JV? Isn't it Better to Keep All of the Profits?

If you have the skills, doing deals yourself is the most profitable way to invest, even if you have to borrow all the money to do it. Whenever you JV, you have to share the profits – so when you look at the figures it seems crazy to do it. Looking at the figures alone will not help you to see the whole picture as it is hard to factor risk into the equation.

Earlier this year my wife and I had close to a million pounds of borrowings, not including mortgages. This was made up of bridging loans, personal loans from friends and family and other investors. We have a great team so are able to handle multiple projects. Although all of the deals we were finding were great and we had a substantial portfolio to back them up, if you are taking out loans to fund 100% of the value of each deal and the refurbishment, you can put yourself and the lender at risk. Each loan you take out has a deadline and managing them all can be a juggling act. If you have 100% borrowing on multiple projects and things go wrong, you can get yourself into trouble if a project runs over on time or budget, or if you have empty rooms and don't make the rental profits you expect. Remember, when building a portfolio mitigating risks is key; you don't want to chase too many deals and risk losing the lot.

In this situation I believe JV's are a great way to continue to invest. The JV partner will input the money either as a hands free investment or as a route to investing for themselves. I like to keep everything as simple as possible: the JV partner will fund 100% of the deposit, the fees and the refurbishment, and will get this money back when the property is refinanced. Generally we would refinance when the project is complete and the property rented. We would have significantly increased the value of the property through the refurbishment and would then borrow 70%-75% of the property's new value depending on what mortgage product we select. Through this first round of refinancing we would expect to get 30%-70% of the investor's money back. The property would then be refinanced when the value has increased enough to get the investor's remaining money out. This would be expected within three to five years but of course there are no guarantees. During this time the investor would achieve 12.5%+ return on the cash they have tied up. Even after refinancing the property, 25%-30% equity would still be created through the refurbishment and gained through property price increases.

Exit Plan

People's circumstances change and whereas you may start out expecting to own the property together, you need to work out what will happen if one party wants to sell. Both parties will have a significant amount of equity in the property and may want to release this through selling or refinancing. You need to set out upfront what will happen if one party wants to sell or refinance. In my view it's not fair to force someone to remain invested in a property long term against their wishes, so I would advise that if either party wants to sell, the other has the option to buy their share at full market value. If the remaining partner does not want to buy the other out, the property must be sold. It is only fair that reasonable notice periods are in place to allow the buyer to raise the funds. You may have a similar agreement in place if either party wanted to refinance to raise funds.

When Not to Joint Venture

I only tend to do JV's on standard run-of-the-mill property deals that I am very confident about, as these are the lowest risk investments. If I am doing something that I have not done before, like converting a commercial property into a block of flats, I would not do it as a

JV. Whenever you do something for the first time, there may be delays or cost overruns to which I would not want to subject a JV partner. I would also be wary of doing a JV if I needed to obtain planning permission for the proposed development. JV partners can be enthusiastic and ignore the risks involved, but I'm sure they would often blame you if things went wrong.

I would also not do a JV if the deal were too good. For example, I have secured a lot of properties using lease option contracts, where the investment is low and the returns often over 100% ROI. My highest ROI for one of these properties was 900%, and I have since bought this property for £296,000 in the same year that the property directly opposite sold for £492,000. On deals like this I think it would be crazy to JV unless you have no other option.

Joint Venturing to Gain Experience

You will learn so much more by doing deals than you will ever learn in a classroom or seminar, but going it alone can be risky, costly and time-consuming. One of the best ways to learn how to invest is to work with someone who is already doing it. This way you get to experience the project first hand and ask all the questions that you wish to gain a full understanding. By doing this you can learn from all the experience of the expert that you work with.

Every property we do is better than the last – we have been learning how to improve things for the last seven years. Some recent improvements we have made have been to put keypad locks on the doors to ensure we never get maintenance callouts when tenants lose their keys. On the last project we developed a way to access all of the plumbing for the en-suites without having to rip bathrooms apart if there is a leak. To maximise your success you need to learn from other people's successes and mistakes rather than reinventing the wheel. If you JV on one or two projects you would then be in a strong position to do your own deals. If you're really wise you may be able to negotiate with your JV partner for them to help you oversee the first project you do on your own. When choosing a JV partner, it is essential that you get on well with them and also important to find someone who can both communicate and teach.

Tim's Deal

One day out of the blue, whilst renovating the house that I would be moving into for the short term, I got a phone call from an investor called Tim who had just started the Simon Zutshi's Mastermind programme (you may remember Tim from earlier in the book where I described how he had a stressful job as a GP and used this as motivation to build a portfolio quickly). Tim was also based in Bristol and was sick of being a GP. He explained that he loved to help people, but having to see one patient every ten minutes throughout the day and deal with all the paperwork had become stressful.

Tim approached me because he knew I had been doing HMO's in Bristol for years and he really wanted to fast-track his results. Tim had some cash to invest so we agreed a plan where we would JV on a couple of deals that he would fund. I would source the property, design the layout to maximise the rent, make it a desirable place to live, and oversee the refurbishment, furnishing, etc. Whilst doing this I would teach him through each deal that we did together and also through the deals that I was doing myself and with other JV partners.

Tim enjoys beer and rugby, which also helped things along and made our meetings a bit more fun. We have now done two great deals together and I wanted him to write about them in his own words. Unfortunately for you, the reader, Tim has agreed four more deals since the two we did together and now has no time to write a case study, so I'll give you a brief outline:

Deal 1 – Ten-bedroom HMO, Bath Road

Purchase price	£369,000
Deposit	£110,700
Stamp duty	£8,450
Solicitor costs	£1,000
Refurbishment	£65,000
Total investment	**£185,150**
Tim's investment	£135,150
Additional investment from friend of family	£50,000
Value when complete	£495,000
New mortgage	£346,500
Tim's cash left in the deal	£97,100
Rent	**£5,325**
Monthly Costs	
Mortgage	£1,546
Bills	£600
Management	£260
Maintenance	£100

Total Cost	**£2,506**
Monthly Profit	**£2,819**
Annual profit	**£33,828**
Tim's 50% share	**£16,914**
Tim's ROI	**17.45%**

This was a great deal. 17.45% is about ten times what Tim would have got in the bank had he put this money in a savings account. This deal would have been even better if we had got the 75% mortgage we were promised right up until the week of the survey, when the bank changed their mind and only agreed to lend 70% of the value because of the size of the property and the number of sharers. With the 75% loan to value, Tim would have £25,000 less tied up in the deal and his ROI would have been 23.51%. Not only does Tim get this great rental return, he also gets half of the equity growth as the property goes up in value too. Equity growth is hard to predict and is no way guaranteed, but even at a conservative 6% growth Tim's share would be £15,000 per annum, making his total profit £31,914 including rental profit and equity growth.

Deal 2 - Seven-bedroom HMO, Bath Road

Purchase Price	£198,000
Deposit	£59,400
Stamp duty	£1,980
Solicitor Costs	£1,000
Architect	£1,000
Building regulations	£450

Refurbishment including loft extension	£70,000
Total investment	**£133,830**
Tim's investment	£83,830
Additional investment from friend of family	£50,000
Value when complete	£350,000
New mortgage	£262,500
Tim's cash left in the deal	£9,930
Rent	**£3,700**
Monthly Costs	
Mortgage	£1,093
Bills	£450
Management	£185
Maintenance	£100
Total Cost	**£1,828**
Monthly Profit	**£1,872**
Annual profit	**£22,464**
Tim's 50% share	**£11,232**
Tim's ROI (yes … Tim will get all his money back within twelve months)	**113.11%**

Tim's total rental profit between these two deals is £28,146, and that's just his share. From two deals he will make an annual profit which is greater than the national average salary in this country!

Icing on the Cake

There is an extremely large garden on the back of the ten-bedroom HMO and many of the neighbouring properties have built on their back gardens. Tim and I intend to build a three-bedroom house in the garden and then turn this into a six-bedroom HMO once built. If we are able to get planning and achieve this intention, we will be able to build the property and refinance every penny that Tim has invested, meaning that both of us will have an infinite ROI.

Working with Tim has been a great pleasure. He and his wife Klare have become good friends and Tim has even cooked us a couple of great roasts. He has been so successful because he set himself a very clear goal (to replace his salary), and has been very decisive when it comes to committing to deals. Tim has made significant investments but through the value we have added to the properties, he has been able to refinance to get back half of the funds that he has invested. Since doing these two deals together, Tim has gone on to do some great deals himself with just a little bit of guidance. He has successfully replaced his GP salary – which is not easy by any stretch of the imagination.

Joint Venture Check List

When looking to invest with a JV partner in order to learn, you should consider the following questions:

Do you like them?

Do you trust them?

Do they have enough experience?

Do they have references?

Are they financially free?

Can they teach as well as do?

Do they have a contract?

Do they have a good team?

Systemising the Process

Debbie Williams, a good friend of mine and a very successful investor, has a tried and tested process for raising JV funding. Debbie is now financially free and spends her time between London and Ibiza where she has just created an amazing second home. After some persuasion, Debbie has agreed to share this process to help you to raise funds for your own ventures. As Debbie explains below, funding is the life blood of many property investors.

So You Have Decided that a Joint Venture Partnership is for You – But How do You get Started?

Many property investors spend huge amounts of personal time speaking with lots of different people who say they are interested in investing, but frustratingly, it does not lead to an actual investment.

So what can you do to use your time more effectively and convert this interest into actual money to support your deals?

Below is a 4-step process to work through so that the JV partnership is successful and profitable for both of you.

1. Qualifying the right JV partner

It is vitally important that you spend some time understanding what would be a great fit for you as a JV partner. This is especially critical when you may work with this individual for a number of years and be partnered on projects involving a lot of capital investment. Taking the time up front to really understand the right partnership for you will pay dividends.

Answering some of the questions earlier in the chapter is a great start. Make sure that you are very clear on your ultimate outcome/vision/goal and indeed why you are seeking a JV partner. Ask yourself: what will the JV partnership give you? And why is this important to you? Be clear about what you want from a JV partner, e.g. solely finance? Or finance and experience/expertise? What kind of expertise? Are you seeking an opportunity to learn from the other person? How will that work? Etc. Think about what you don't want from a JV Partner as well. Knowing what you are ***not*** *seeking in a partner is just as important as knowing what you want. It helps to keep the conversations on point and relevant so you do not waste each other's valuable time.*

Any relationship can be challenging. If your values are not aligned with those of the other person, it can lead to friction, discontent and differing expectations. Take time to understand your own top three values and why these are important to you. You can then evaluate your potential JV partner, checking in on whether your values will be met or complemented in such a partnership.

A key deciding factor is – could you work with this person, especially when things go wrong?

2. Finding potential JV partners

Many property investors frequently ask where they can find JV partners. The obvious places are property networking meetings, which can be very valuable meet-ups for many reasons. However, they are also competitive environments, where a number of property investors are seeking finance. Consequently, it can make securing finance a little more difficult and the rewards that potential partners expect, whether percentage return on cash loans or share of rental profits/capital equity, can be higher than outside of the property network.

When I first started to raise finance in October 2012, I spent three months meeting with anyone who expressed an interest. It was completely random and a huge waste of personal time in terms of travel and meeting time. It did not lead to any money.

In January 2013, I completely changed my approach to a much more strategic, well thought through process. This led to me raising £1 million in four months!

Firstly, start to look at your own personal networks. This may include friends, family, work colleagues, your own business networks, the golf club, hobbies and other social networks. You may also know people who don't necessarily have the funds to invest themselves, or would not be interested, but they may be very well-connected and could perhaps refer you to other people who would be potential investors.

Create a shortlist of who you will target to open up a conversation about whether they are interested in an opportunity to earn greater rewards on their cash. Don't narrow your list to just those people that you know who have cash. There are many other criteria that you need to consider before a name makes the shortlist. This includes questions such as – what is their appetite for investing? Have they invested before? If so, in what? E.g. property, stocks and shares, bonds, etc.? What was their experience? What is their attitude to sharing risk/reward? How comfortable are they with change? How do they react to problems? These are just some of the questions to consider.

I have a personal friend who has in excess of £100,000 sitting in the bank. She did not make my shortlist because I know she is extremely cautious and whilst property investment could earn her great returns, I know she would not be comfortable with the risk aspect. Do not just focus on the availability of funds – this is very short-sighted and may lead to a bad selection of JV partner and problems further down the line.

Once you have completed a list of up to twenty-five individuals, this should become your sole focus. Focus and discipline drives results. Track each of your communications carefully in an Excel spreadsheet so you know when you spoke to them, what was discussed, what the outcome was, the agreed next steps, date/time of your next conversation and any actions required. Without this, it will be difficult to stay on top of your progress professionally and effectively.

3. Engaging JV partners

I would recommend that the first engagement you have with a potential JV partner is a telephone conversation of up to thirty minutes. I use this as an opportunity to qualify the interest before committing to a face to face meeting.

Initial telephone call

Do not discuss any deals or rates of return in the initial conversation. Do take a few minutes to give a very high level overview of your property success to date, where you invest, what your investment strategies are and what it has given you. The primary objective of the call is to gain a better understanding of why the individual is potentially interested in investing in property, so you can appreciate their agenda to see if you can indeed help them or not. Ask what they are looking to achieve by investing; what their experience is of this type of investment to date, if any; what their expectations are; and when they are thinking about investing. The information that can be gleaned in the initial call can help you to qualify the character of the person as a potential business partner as well as establish their current means and their level of intent to proceed.

The outcome of the telephone call will determine whether you take the conversation any further or not at this stage. If it seems that the person could be a great candidate and it has the potential to be a successful and enjoyable partnership for both of you, commit to a sixty-minute face to face coffee meeting and schedule it with them while on the call.

Face to face coffee meeting

In advance of a face to face meeting, make sure you are fully prepared. First impressions count, so arrive at the venue early and present yourself in a smart but friendly manner.

Preparing in advance with a professional, branded presentation, as well as branded factsheets to give to the potential JV partner at the end of the session will demonstrate that you are valuing his/her time, that you are credible and serious about how you operate as a professional investor.

A winning pitch should include a distinct mission statement of what you are offering, why they should invest with you, a summary of your investment strategies/locations, investment options, case studies, how the JV partnership will work and next steps from here. Walk them through an example of a typical investment business case so they understand the level of investment, the level of return and the timescale. Step into the shoes of the potential JV investor and ensure that you address all of the questions and concerns that may be running through their minds. The JV partner is looking for certainty, trust, professionalism, proven track record and a clear investment proposition.

Use the face to face session to build rapport and to flush out all of the questions and concerns. Ensure the potential JV investor walks away with a clear understanding/appreciation of who you are, what you bring to the table, your professionalism, your knowledge and confidence to achieve desired results.

Give the potential JV partner a number of professionally produced materials such as a profile overview, a next steps guide and an investor testimonial sheet to take away and read at leisure.

Follow-up telephone call / second follow-up call

At the end of the coffee meeting, advise the potential investor that you will give them a few days to absorb all of the information and then you will follow up with a call to see if they have any further questions or concerns. The intention here is to ensure that there is nothing further on their mind that may be holding them back from investing and moving forward.

It may be necessary to have a second call. However, by then, the individual has had ample opportunity to cover all of their points and I proceed to get a commitment from them to invest or not.

Commitment to proceed

Upon a successful commitment to proceed, I put the appropriate legal paperwork in place and kick off the process to start to source an appropriate deal to make the profitable investment for both of us a reality.

It is critical to manage communication and expectations carefully as you move forward. Inform the JV partner how frequently you will be giving status updates and via what method (normally email). Get buy-in that this is acceptable to them or work out a compromise. Put in place a consistent structured approach to communications, so the JV partner does not get cold feet or start to make incorrect assumptions about what is actually happening.

4. Nurturing the ongoing relationship

If you have invested time in qualifying and engaging with a JV partner who is a great fit, but he/she is not ready to invest right now, it is important that you continue to nurture the interest. Maybe they are waiting for a bonus from work or some inheritance money, for example.

Keeping the interest alive requires you to think about the frequency of contact you need to have and what you will say/share. If that person is potentially a very important investor to you, keep in touch with them perhaps bi-weekly or once a month; similarly, keep in touch with your backup investors at monthly or bi-monthly intervals. You do not want to stalk the potential JV partner so you need to have friendly check-ins alongside sharing something of value. This might be interesting and relevant property investment articles, latest case studies, interesting property market statistics, latest deals you have secured, etc. Whatever you decide to share, it needs to be relevant, it needs to build on your rapport and continue to give the JV partner confidence and certainty that investing with you is absolutely the right decision.

Raising finance is, for most people, the life blood of their property portfolio and being able to raise sufficient funds when you need them is critical to portfolio growth and achieving your dreams. It is the difference between securing great deals or not. Invest the time to qualify, source, engage and convert the interest successfully. Do not wait until you have a deal: start to raise finance now so you can move swiftly when the best deals do come up.

As you can see Debbie has really got this part of the process nailed down. She is now raising money from Ibiza to put into some of our projects, which allows me to focus on finding the properties and maximising their potential. With Debbie on the team I'm sure we'll be doing even more deals. She now runs hugely successful workshops specifically about this process and I can highly recommend her. To find out more about her courses please email her: debbie@mypropertyangels.com.

Summary

When investing with other people's money, it is imperative to treat it with the utmost respect. Only do great deals with a really high return and never do a deal that you wouldn't do with your own money. Don't do anything that is high risk with someone else's money, and at the same time make sure the investor is aware of the risks.

Investing responsibly with other people's money is a great way to increase your income and wealth as well as the investor's; these deals should be truly win-win. It would be wise to borrow money for some deals so that you maximise your profits and keep all the equity, balancing this with some 50:50 JV's where the risk and reward is shared, and there are no short deadlines by when you need to return the funds. Although this will reduce your profit, it is a much more stable way to grow your business.

Chapter 15: Investing With Others And Making It Safe

"*As safe as houses*"

Unknown

Do You Have Time to Do it Yourself?

It's takes a lot of blood sweat and tears to get good at anything; to get good at doing big deals is a massive learning curve. It's very easy to read a book like this in a few hours and think it's easy. In this book I have simplified and condensed my learning to give the reader a flavour of what it takes to become a big deal investor. This journey is not for everyone. Often people don't have the time required for such a journey and prefer the idea of property investment without going through all of the pain. It is possible to invest with other property investors but even this way there can be a lot of pitfalls, or at least things to consider.

Maybe you do want to invest yourself but would like to invest with someone more experienced first so that you can learn the ropes whilst still generating an income. This can be a great idea because you learn so much more by doing, compared with what you will ever learn from a book or in a seminar or classroom. Not only can you learn more but your confidence can grow massively with the right experience and you will feel a lot more comfortable when taking on the challenge of your own deal.

Whether you want to become a hands free investor or want to do a deal with someone else to learn how to do it yourself, there are a number of things to consider when investing with another individual or company. This chapter will address what you need to take into account.

Who to Invest with

Someone you get on with

When I got sacked a few years back and decided never to work for anyone else ever again, I realised that never again would I have to work with people I didn't want to. I'm lucky in that I can now choose who I spend my time with. This was a very liberating feeling and since then I've only worked with the best people. Business and investing should be a fun, or at least an enjoyable, experience so when choosing who to invest with, selecting partners you will get on well with is really important.

A proven track record

When choosing someone to invest with, it is best to go for a person with experience. Investing is such a steep learning curve that it can be quite risky to invest with somebody who is just starting out. Cost overruns, months of delays and so on can all be very expensive and vastly reduce the return on investment that you were promised at the start of the project. In the worst cases you could even lose some or all of the investment capital that you put into the deal. There are always risks with investing but working with somebody who has completed numerous investments similar to the one that you are undertaking vastly reduces the risk. Someone like this will already have experienced the common obstacles and pitfalls, will have dealt with the Planning and Building Regulations departments and should know what's required.

Someone with financial backing

Investing with someone who has financial back-up can give peace of mind. When investing it's always important to use contracts which can be used to protect you if things go wrong. If the person that you invest with doesn't meet their side of the bargain, you can then claim compensation through mediation or through the courts; but if the person that you invest with is broke or even bankrupt, it will be very difficult to get financial recourse. Even if a court orders that they pay you, it's likely to be at a rate of about £10 a week and will frustrate the hell out of you if you let it. If you invest with somebody who has a property portfolio, they will do everything they can to protect their credit rating. The last thing they will want is a county court judgement against their name, as this will stop them getting mortgages in the future.

Is it best to invest with a company or an individual?

Many people think it is safer to invest in a company than in an individual. Although a company may seem like a professional outfit, the owners are not liable for the company's debts. Therefore it is possible for the directors to put their company into liquidation (close it down) and not be responsible for paying you back. In this worst case scenario, you would be left trying to fight the appointed receiver to try to get your money; after the receivers have taken their fee, there may not be any left to claim.

I suggest either investing with/lending to an individual, or if investing with/lending to a company then insist on a personal guarantee from the owners to repay the debt if the company folds.

This way you can pursue them for the money. It is also wise to check that the company owners have some financial backing – such as savings or equity in property, since nearly anybody can set up a company.

A one man band or a team?

Many people start out as a one man band because this is the best way to keep the costs down, so in the early days an investor is responsible for the renovation, the lettings, the maintenance, the accounts, the cleaning, etc. I started out working with a good friend and we had to do everything ourselves. The truth is that most of the jobs we were not very good at so we were so glad when we were able to start employing others.

When there were two of us we could always rely on each other and support each other if one of us was away. A mentoring client of mine was recently about to do a joint venture with an individual who needed investment. Before the purchase went through the guy came down with a stress-related illness and had to take time out for a few months. My client was forced to abandon the project and was very lucky that it didn't happen after the property was bought. It's not really a nice thing to think about, but when investing a lot of money it is necessary to consider what would happen if something were to happen to the person that you are investing with midway through a project. For this reason I think it's advisable to invest in a team rather than a one man band.

Security

When making any sizeable investment, it would be wise to secure the investment against an asset owned by the person to whom you are lending the money. This can be done in a number of ways:

A first legal charge

Usually a mortgage company would have the first charge on a property as they are the first to lend and generally have the highest value of loan. If the property is being bought for cash with no mortgage, then you can request a first legal charge against the property as security. In the event of a repossession, the first charge lender gets all of their money back before any other lender can get theirs. The owner of the property must also get the first charge lender's permission before they can secure any other loans against the property.

For these reasons the first charge lender is in a very strong position and this is why it is best to get a first charge as security if at all possible. You don't necessarily need to get a charge against the property being bought – you can secure the loan against other property owned by the borrower. When loaning money it is important to ensure that the asset being used as security is worth at least as much as the loan. High street lenders, for example, often only lend 90% of the value of a property for two reasons:

a) because they want the borrower to use some of their own money so they have something at stake if things go wrong.
b) because they know that if they need to repossess, then there will be fees to pay before they get their money.

As a first charge lender you may repossess the property within the terms of the loan agreement if the seller defaults on their payments.

A second legal charge

If there is already a first charge on the property you may secure your loan as a second legal charge. You will need the first charge lender's permission to do this, which is something that your solicitor will need to obtain. A second legal charge is still strong security; however you will be behind the first charge lender in the queue to get your money back if the house is repossessed.

As a second charge lender you may repossess the property within the terms of the loan agreement if the seller defaults on their payments. You will however need the permission of the first charge lender to do so.

The owner could not add a third charge lender without your permission.

A restriction on the property title

A restriction is another way to secure a loan against the property title. Having a restriction stops the property owner (the borrower) from selling or remortgaging the property without your permission. This effectively secures your equity by tying up the asset so that the owner can't sell or remortgage without paying you back. You do not need the other lender's permission to apply a restriction, which does make this approach a lot quicker and simpler.

The drawback with a restriction is that it does not allow you to repossess the property to get your money back. So although the money is secure in that the asset can't be sold, there may be long delays before getting your money back.

A loan agreement

A loan agreement is a contract between the lender and the borrower which is signed by both parties and witnessed by independent parties. This contract is often written by a solicitor and then checked by the other party's solicitor. This document contains all of the key terms of the loan including:

- The lender's full name and address
- The borrower's full name and address
- The amount being lent
- The length of the loan
- The interest to be paid
- The security (if any) being provided for the loan
- What will happen if the borrower defaults on interest payments
- What will happen if the borrower defaults on the repayment of the loan at the end of the term.

The loan agreement is often used in conjunction with the first charge, the second charge or the restriction, and can be lodged with the Land Registry along with the charge documentation.

Is a contract really necessary?

I highly recommend using a contract. Even with the best of intentions things can go very wrong and it is imperative that both parties are protected in case they do. Contracts also help you clarify exactly what the relationship is and the terms of the agreement. If you have discussed an investment with someone but have not put pen to paper, it is very likely that you may have missed something or end up walking away with differing expectations about what has been agreed.

A word of warning about solicitors

Solicitors who are not used to dealing with these kinds of things can be very pessimistic. That's not their fault; it's just their job to point out all potential hazards when investing money. It is not their job to help you get wealthy. This is not a problem if you are prepared for it; listen to what they say and make up your own mind.

This is also something to be aware of when borrowing funds. If you have found somebody who wants to lend you money for your deal, you need to fully explain what will happen and when, and you need to run through each part of the loan agreement with them. Once you have done this, answered all of their questions and they are comfortable with it all, you then need to explain the solicitor's role. You need to warn them in advance that the solicitor may well be negative or pessimistic, and that they will point out all of the pitfalls. Explain that if they don't do this, they wouldn't be doing their job properly. You should also explain that most solicitors don't understand the benefits of investing and that the return you are offering is great, and also remind them that you are offering security, etc. If you do this properly, it gives you a lot of credibility when the solicitor does exactly what you say they will do. It shows that you know what you're talking about, you have experience and are not just trying to pull a fast one.

Due diligence

It is essential to do due diligence on every property deal before you invest. The person who has found the deal may be unrealistic about the cost of the work or the timescales – or some may even deliberately try to make a deal sound better than it is to get you to invest. You are 100% responsible for your money at all times and should ask a lot of questions before deciding to invest. You should apply everything you have learnt through this book to ensure it's a great deal. You should be looking at the risks, how likely they are and how severe the outcome. You should look into what has been done to mitigate the risks. You should ask about the Plan B – what happens if you don't get planning? What if the costs overrun? What happens if the property is down-valued following all the work? If the person has done this before, they should be able to show you case studies on paper as well as properties. We generally have two to three projects running at any one time so are able to take potential investors around properties at various stages of development. If the investor is interested we can show them the finished project before they make a decision.

References

It is always least risky to work with someone who has experience. Anyone who has experience should be able to provide references to give you peace of mind. Make sure you check out the references and speak to the person who has given the reference.

Trust your gut

After doing your due diligence you need to assess both the person and the investment to see if you can work with them. When you do this, however, do not rely solely on the facts and figures presented. You need to listen to your body. If your gut says no then you have to walk away, even if the deal is great on paper. The human body and the subconscious mind are wiser than you can ever imagine. Your subconscious mind observes millions and millions of bits of information that you're not even aware of; it has been working your whole life and its main job is to help you stay safe. If your gut says "*No, don't do the deal,*" don't question it, just trust it. To do a deal, both your head and your gut need to say yes.

Summary

Property is a great investment but it takes a lot of experience to get good at investing. Be realistic about whether you *have* the time, and whether learning to be a property investor is the *best use* of your time. If you can create money elsewhere through your profession but are time-limited, then investing your funds with someone else might be the best way forward for you. Your money is your responsibility and you must do your own due diligence for any deal you consider investing in. Invest with someone who has a track record, who can give references, and can show you their work. Make sure you have contracts and get them checked by a solicitor. You should also make sure that your money is secured against the property with a charge or, as a minimum, a restriction against the title.

Chapter 16:
Get Out There And Make It Happen

"Don't wait until the iron is hot; make the iron hot by striking."

William B. Sprague

Your Next Steps – Putting it all into Action

Hopefully now you've read this book you will be feeling it's time to take your property investing to the next level. I sincerely hope that you have taken some notes but most importantly made lots of action points to help you put a plan together. I'm sure some of you may be feeling a little overwhelmed since a £1 million deal that produces £58,000 annual profit may seem a long way from where you are right now. It was not a giant leap for me from a standing start to a massive deal. I got to where I am by taking little steps every week to move me in the direction of my goals. I started with a small deal and just got a little bit bigger each time. In this section, I want to break down the steps that you will need to take to become a big deal investor.

Your next step will depend very much on where you are within your property journey. It would be foolish to think about your first deal being a nineteen-bedroom block of flats; it's all about stepping stones. For someone with little experience in HMO's it may be wise to start with a Rent to Rent deal; this way you wouldn't have to go through all the hassle of buying and setting up the property. Take some time now to write an action plan to get you from where you are to where you want to be.

Stage 1 - Make a Plan

It's time to make a plan! Dreams without action plans are just dreams and will never come true. Take some time now to work out what your next steps should be and if you haven't already done this, put them into the action plan at the back of this book. If you need a helping hand I've written a summary at the end of each chapter in Part 2 to help jog your memory.

Stage 2 - Get it in Your Diary

Having an action plan in the back of this book is a great start but unless you keep this book with you it's pretty much useless. Copy your action plan to somewhere where you have access to it all the time – maybe on your phone. Next up, take the action plan and put the action items into your diary to make sure they happen.

Stage 3 - Get an Accountability Buddy

This is someone on the same or a similar journey. Basically you talk on the phone to make sure you're both taking action; you support each other through the ups and downs and knock-backs, and kick each other's ass if one of you doesn't take action.

Stage 4 – Create a Power Team

Who do you need in your power team? Make a list and then set about finding the key players you need for legal, financial, planning permission and investing advice.

Stage 5 – Get a Mentor

Find someone who inspires you, who you can teach you. Find someone who has achieved what you want to achieve.

Stage 6 – Find Your Hidden Treasure

If you have rental properties you may well be sitting on hidden treasure. One of the quickest ways you can increase cash flow is through changing your single let properties into house shares/HMO's. You may also want to consider extending properties or converting loft space to living space to add both rental income and value.

Stage 7 – Get Out and Find Your Next Deal

Start searching RightMove, paying particular attention to the floor plans. Work out how to maximise the space in each property to maximise the rent and the value.

Stage 8 – Organise Your Funding

Establish where your deposit and refurbishment funds will come from. Speak to brokers about who will be prepared to give you a mortgage.

Stage 9 – Get it Refurbished/Converted

Find a great builder that you can work well with, and explain what you need to achieve and the time scales. Make sure you get everything written down to avoid having to pay for extras.

Stage 10 – Get it Rented

Dress the property to impress and start conducting viewings. Group viewings will really help to get people to agree to rent the property – they will fear missing out. Make sure you get maximum rents to maximise your profits and also maximise the property value.

Stage 11 – Get it Refinanced

Refinance the property to recoup as much of your investment as possible so that you're in the best position possible for your next deal.

Stage 12 – Find the Next Deal

Look for a deal bigger and better than your last one. This next deal should be a stepping stone in the direction of doing deals that make £50,000-£100,000 profit per annum. Repeat the process for this deal.

Extra Resources

Free webinar – Rent to Rent and Lease Options

To help you move forward faster with Rent to Rent and lease options strategies, I have developed a webinar which I have decided to give away for free as a gift to you for buying my book. On the webinars I will explain why Rent to Rent and lease options are a great strategy and how you can get started with little to no money.

www.retireononepropertydeal.co.uk/free

Free webinar - Retire on One Deal

For those of you interested in making really big money, I have developed the *Retire on One Deal* webinar which again I will give for free as a gift for buying this book. In this great webinar I go through what it takes to be a big deal investor, going from just getting by in property to making big money from every deal.

www.retireononepropertydeal.co.uk/webinar

HMO Tours

There's only so much you can learn in a book or even in a classroom. Seeing everything on paper or in a presentation feels so theoretical that people can find it hard to take what they have learnt and put it into action. There is a massive void between the theory and the practice; for example, if you read a book about cycling would you expect to be able to ride a bike without falling off? No, I thought not!

This is why I have decided to run HMO tours to allow people to see the properties 'in the flesh' and understand how to maximise the rent whilst still providing good quality accommodation. Seeing the properties really helps to bring the theory to life, which then takes you a step further to implementing things yourself. During the HMO tours I take the group around the current projects and explain why we selected each property, how much we paid, how much we're spending on each property. We do a presentation at the end to run through the deals and talk through the advantages of investing in HMO's. We also do a question and answer session to answer your queries so that you can put what you've learned into practice in your own portfolio.

www.retireononepropertydeal.co.uk/hmotour

Home study courses

To find out details of home study courses:

www.retireononepropertydeal.co.uk/homestudy

Summary

It's time to get out there and make it happen. Follow the steps in this chapter to help you make a plan of attack. Use the end of chapter summaries to remind yourself of the key points you have learnt through this book.

Chapter 17:
Accelerate Your Success

"*Your mentors in life are important, choose them wisely.*"

Robert Kiyosaki (Rich Dad)

Case Study – Mark's Deal, Lease Option in Cardiff

Mark is one of my mentoring clients who has really taken the bull by the horns and taken loads of action with lease options following what I taught him and his team. Mark's first deal during the mentorship was a ten-bedroom lease option that makes well over £1,500 per month. Since then he has agreed many Rent to Rent and lease option deals and is currently negotiating a deal on a portfolio of six large HMO's, each with eight to ten bedrooms. This portfolio alone is enough to replace even the biggest of salaries. I'll let Mark tell you about it in his own words:

I have been investing in property for almost fifteen years now, starting with two-up, two-down refurbishments in the north of England before establishing my own lettings business, selling it and relocating to Pembrokeshire. Over that time I have seen dramatic changes in the property market. The financial crisis of 2007 changed the landscape of property, and new and innovative solutions were required for investors like myself to carry on in our chosen profession and continue to acquire property.

In 2008 I established my rent assist company, UK Contractor Lettings, and began to lease properties from tired landlords and let them on a room by room basis to companies looking to accommodate their workforces here in the UK. It was a great business but at the end of a company contract we would simply hand the properties back to the landlords and lose our ability to monetise the building. I remember thinking to myself that there had to be a way of extending the lifecycle of these deals, which is where Barry Davies came in.

Barry was carrying out presentations around the Pin network's regular meetings. He was helping people with their property businesses and so I bought his book Escape the Rat Race, *which provided accurate and actionable advice; I could see how the implementation of his lease option strategy would make my business bigger and better than it already was.*

After a brief meeting he agreed to help my company and began to train my team to source, negotiate and close lease option deals that could be used for multi-let purposes. Where we were once only generating cash flow, we were now going to acquire major equity stakes in large buildings circa £300,000. It was exciting.

The first property that we sourced with him was on Cowbridge Road, Cardiff; it was essentially three apartments carved out of an old Victorian building and located in Cardiff City centre. The landlord had a number of smaller properties and this one was proving to be too much for him to cope with. He was a part time landlord, working elsewhere, and the property was simply a headache for him in terms of maintenance and tenants and so he was ready to park it up for the long term or sell ... a perfect lease option opportunity.

The property was tired, and a gap in the render had allowed damp to penetrate through the walls and turn the interior an unattractive black. It was never going to let out like this. The apartments themselves were split into two x two-bedrooms and one x three-bedroom, all with their own kitchens and bathrooms. It required a little bit of love and after agreeing a fixed price with the landlord to purchase in the future, a monthly lease fee and a small option fee, we quickly signed the deal, which is outlined here:

Purchase price	*£340,000*
Option fee	*£500*
Lease fee pcm	*£1,200*
Term	*7 years*
Total cost of works (including furnishings)	*£16,000*
Current market value	*£315,000*
Number of lettable rooms	*8*
Market rent per room pcm	*£400*
Total estimated rent pcm	*£3,200*
Utilities, etc., pcm	*£600*
Net rental profit pcm (rent - lease fee - bills)	*£1,400*

We had secured an asset that not only gave us an amazing monthly cash flow, but had also secured the equity gain on the property over the next seven years, which we hoped would equate to somewhere in the region of £150,000.

The training continued, and our team continued to develop their skills in sourcing and acquiring larger properties with huge potential for multi-let, with the most recent acquisition consisting of a small portfolio of six properties with a value of circa £2.5 million currently progressing to refurbishment.

Barry's expertise was key in identifying the right properties and he has an intuitive understanding of how a deal will stack up and the optimum layout for maximising your return. Since starting to work with him I have watched him move on to bigger and more impressive deals and hope to continue to leverage his experience and advice for as long as he is happy to allow me.

Working with Mark and his team has been great – they are so proactive it's hard keeping track of what they are up to. Mark himself is very skilled at systemising things, which makes it very easy for him and his team to do multiple deals at once. Mark has run a very successful corporate letting and relocation business for years and now he is securing these properties for the long term, not only creating great cash flow but significant capital gains through the market growth of the properties too. I knew I'd found a good guy when I felt that I was learning as much out of our discussions as Mark was. Mark has now started teaching Rent to Rent and I'd highly recommend his course. (Contact him on mark@intelligenthg.co.uk for details.)

Educate Yourself

Getting the right education and support is key to building a successful property business.

We have specialised in investing in HMO's using lease option contracts and also joint venture agreements for six years, mastering the art of securing large, high value, high cash-flowing properties using little of our own money. I started out in property full time with one disastrous property behind me and £8,500 in the bank. I had been sacked for running a property business, but the property business I was trying to launch wasn't making any money. Since then, we have built a multi-million property portfolio; our total profit is £24,000 per month although we reinvest most of it.

I love sharing my experience and the knowledge that I have gained and have been running courses and mentoring programmes for the last five years. I really enjoy helping others to invest in property – it's great to see people take control of their lives and become financially free. It's not the money they make that gives me the buzz, it's more the choices that it opens up for them and also the confidence that it gives them. When people achieve results better than they ever thought possible in property, it makes them re-evaluate everything. If they can achieve this in property, what can they achieve elsewhere in their lives?

Through the five years I have spent as a trainer and a mentor, it has been really important to me not to be 'just another property trainer'. I'm not one of those guys with a massive ego who loves the sound of his own voice and can't wait to get on stage. For me training is all about the people in the room and how we can best serve them. One of the first things I noticed through participating in trainings is that lots of the participants really struggle to take action; they tend to procrastinate either because they're nervous or simply because they're not hungry enough.

When I started training I was adamant that the people I trained would get more than knowledge from me: I decided I would force them to take action. I started by training people in the Rent to Rent strategy. Rather than simply telling people what to say to agents, I would role play the whole script with them; we would then go through all of the most common objections that letting agents and landlords were likely to come up with; and then we'd role play objection handling. This was already much more than most trainers would do but it wasn't enough. I knew that if I left it at that, the vast majority of people still wouldn't take action. The next thing we did was to start calling agents. The moment I announced that it was time to call agents there would be a look of sheer panic on people's faces! The majority of those in the room, about 95%, would take action. Some really got into it and after fifteen minutes of calls it was hard to round everyone up and get them back in the room. Often half of the room would get a positive response from agents and have potential deals lined up with viewings booked for the following Monday or Tuesday. The looks on people's faces when they came back into the room was unbelievable: many chuffed with the fact that they had set up deals, others chuffed that they had faced their fears and made the calls.

One thing that I have learnt is that when people have done something once, it's much easier to do it the next time. This was why it was so important to get people to take action during the training. Since this massive success I have ensured that all of my trainings are action-packed and actually get people moving towards their goals. Even this book is based around encouraging the reader to take action, with summaries of chapters for you to refer back to and action points for you to take.

The other key thing I have learnt is that many training programmes focus on speaking at the audience rather than engaging with them and answering specific questions about their deals. Lots of the trainings are in big rooms crammed with people so it's impossible to give real support. For this reason I generally train people in smaller groups so that I can offer more support.

Retire On One Property Deal Seminar (Live One Day Event)

With more and more people interested in investing in HMO's and in bigger deals, we have launched the Retire On One Property Deal workshop, where we go through what it takes to be a big deal investor. We share how you can move from small single let properties to house shares and HMO's that will double, triple or even quadruple your profit per property. For the even more ambitious, we'll go through even bigger deals, including the property with £60,000 annual profit, which would actually allow most people to retire. Although this might seem daunting we will show you the step by step process of getting from where you are now to where you want to be. All you will need to focus on is the next stepping stone.

Big Deal Mentoring Programme

For people who really want to accelerate their growth and make this their best year ever I offer the Big Deal Mentoring Programme. This programme is specifically designed to go through all aspects of becoming a Big Deal Investor.

The key things you need to accelerate your growth are a mentor, a peer group, specific education and regular support. With this in mind I have developed a mentoring program for those who are serious about moving through the stepping stones onto bigger investments and wish to accelerate their journey by leveraging my expertise, my team, and experience.

The program I have developed is unique. Firstly the numbers will be restricted to eight to ten people to create an intimate group. This will ensure each member gets dedicated support tailored individually to them. The mentoring takes the form of a twelve-month programme based around monthly meetings where we give specific training in the mornings and help you through your deals in the afternoons.

You will find details of this and other mentoring programmes on www.retireononepropertydeal.co.uk/mentoring.

Specific training

As part of the group you will receive the most up to date training on the strategies we're using right now to generate £2,000+++ profit per property per month. Through the programme we will explain all the aspects of investing in detail, from working through the numbers, to dealing with planning, through maximising your property right through to dressing and renting your property.

Access to my power team

As part of the mentoring program I will also give you access to my power team. In fact many of them will even be presenting their specific, highly valuable knowledge to the group. This is the power team that I have worked with on the deals that I have done and I have found them to be both knowledgeable and reliable.

Individual support

Each month you will receive support to work on your personal deals and challenges. This will be led by myself with other members of the group sharing their key relevant experience to help you move forward. I have experienced this strong group support as a participant many times and it is one of the most powerful things you can do to help move you forward.

An awesome peer group

If you're selected for the programme you will be surrounded by an excellent group of people on a similar journey to you who will really want you to succeed. Part of the responsibility of being in the group is that you need to commit to supporting the other members of the group to help them achieve their goals too. One of the great things about groups like this is that although most members have a similar mindset, everyone brings their own experiences and skills, which is what makes it so powerful.

Sample programme

The programme will evolve over time but here is a sample of the kind of things that will be included:

Monthly meetings

Session 1 – Sourcing deals

Session 2 – Getting funding

Session 3 – Planning permission

Session 4 – Maximising rental returns

Session 5 – Converting the properties to HMO's/flats

Session 6 – HMO lease options

Session 7 – Getting the highest valuation

Session 8 – Managing mega-HMO's

Session 9 – Joint ventures

Session 10 – Flipping properties

Session 11 – Project management

Session 12 – Buying tax-efficiently

Monthly webinars

Between the monthly meetings we will be holding monthly webinars one evening during the week. In these we will deliver extra content to assist you further with your investing, and also assist you with any questions you have or challenges you face between the monthly meetings.

Facebook group

There will be a private Facebook group set up where you will be able to post your questions as well as share your struggles and successes.

999 calls

Sometimes in property/business you need support fast, for example, if you have a deal that's about to fall over. For these situations we have included "999 calls" where we can arrange a call within twenty-four hours (usually this will be the same day but that's not always possible). These calls are limited but are there for when you really need them.

Who am I looking for?

I'm looking for people who are determined to make this year their best year ever.

I'm looking for people with a massive hunger for success.

I'm looking for people willing to take massive action.

I'm looking for people who already have some property experience.

I'm looking for people with some funds to invest or who can raise some funds to invest in their deals.

Get in Touch

If you want to learn more about how we can work together please get in touch:

barrydaviesproperty.co.uk

barry@barrydaviesproperty.co.uk

facebook.com/HMOLeaseOptions

And Finally ...

I hope you've enjoyed the quotes throughout this book. I've saved my favourite until last to finish on a high.

The Man in the Arena

"*It is not the critic who counts; not the man who points out how the strong man stumbles, or where the doer of deeds could have done them better. The credit belongs to the man who is actually in the arena, whose face is marred by dust and sweat and blood; who strives valiantly; who errs, who comes short again and again, because there is no effort without error and shortcoming; but who does actually strive to do the deeds; who knows great enthusiasms, the great devotions; who spends himself in a worthy cause; who at the best knows in the end the triumph of high achievement, and who at the worst, if he fails, at least fails while daring greatly, so that his place shall never be with those cold and timid souls who neither know victory nor defeat.*"

Theodore Roosevelt

Thank You

Thanks for taking the time to read or listen to this book. Time is your most valuable asset and I'm honoured that you have spent it on this book. I hope you've enjoyed reading it as much as I've enjoyed writing it. Now it's time for you to go out and make it happen. Good luck with your investing! I hope to meet you at a property event some time.

To Your Success!

Barry Davies

Action List

"An ounce of action is worth a ton of theory."

Ralph Waldo Emerson

Action No.	Description	Date
1		
2		
3		
4		
5		
6		
7		
8		
9		
10		
11		

12		
13		
14		
15		
16		
17		
18		
19		
20		

About the Author

Barry Davies is a property investor, speaker, author and mentor. He achieved financial freedom a number of years ago through the multi-million pound property portfolio that he has grown, which now makes hundreds of thousands in rental profits each year.

Passionate about property investing, he loves doing big property deals. Whilst most investors are content to work with properties worth £100,000-£200,000, Barry looks for bigger and better deals to inspire himself and those around him. He has completed his first million pound deal and is now working on his second.

He has inspired thousands of people with his property journey, which he started with £8,500 after being sacked in the middle of a recession, through speaking at events all over the country.

On a personal note, keeping physically fit is paramount. He weight trains two to three times a week, does fitness training twice a week and has even run a couple of marathons. Keen to give any sport or challenge a go, he is always looking for new experiences.

Barry loves to help others achieve their property and financial targets. As he started with nothing, he knows exactly what it's like to go through the challenges his clients face on their own property journeys. The case studies in the book show how he has helped others achieve financial freedom through his mentorship programme.

He continues to follow his passion and still invests to achieve bigger and better goals. Barry loves what he does and has no plans to retire.